Whispering Quilts:
A Slave's Journey of Hope,
Struggle, and Freedom

Copyright Registration #: TX-8-736-480

Quilt illustrations: Richard Haynes © 2017, 2019

Cover Design: Charaf Essbati

ISBN: 9781707923434
Imprint: Independently published, R.M. Tappin

Dedication

In Memory of Marita Haynes

(1953-2017)

To the loving memory of my friend, Marita Haynes, precious wife of Richard Haynes, devoted mother of Stefan, Kristina, and Sabine, and adoring grandmother of ten grandchildren. In breaking loose from chains of mental and emotional oppression that were intended to shackle her to a racist *status quo*, she followed her North Star to love and live with purpose.

Contents

DEDICATION III

PREFACE..VII

FOREWORD..X

INTRODUCTION..1

CHAPTER 1 3

THOMAS' STORY 3

THE ANCESTORS..4

MY MOTHER'S MOTHER: GRANDMOTHER CHARLOTTE...........................5

MY MOTHER'S FATHER: AN UNKNOWN GRANDDADDY.............................9

MY FATHER'S DADDY: GRANDDADDY ISAAC 10

OLD MAMMY 11

CHAPTER 2 14

MARRIAGE AND FAMILY 14

HOME, NOT-SO-SWEET HOME LIFE 16

FAMILY MEALS 20

PUTTIN' ON MASSA 22

WORK LIFE FOR DADDY JAMES..23

WORK LIFE FOR MOTHER CHRISSY 26

MY MOTHER'S SECRETS 29

A BRUTAL PUNISHMENT 33

CHAPTER 3 38

FEAR AND FLIGHT: THE PLANNING 38

THE WAGON WHEEL 48

THE FLYING GEESE...51

CHAPTER 4 .... **54**

THE ESCAPE 54

THE NORTH STAR 57

THE LOG CABIN 62

THE BEAR'S PAW 70

THE BEAR'S PAW QUILT 71

SHOO-FLY 77

THE BOW-TIE 81

DRUNKARD'S PATH 86

CROSSROADS 90

CHAPTER 5 .... **93**

NORTH THROUGH NEW ENGLAND 93

CHAPTER 6 .... **99**

LIFE IN BRITISH CANADA: 1850 – 99

CHAPTER 7 .... **103**

PASSAGES 103

CHAPTER 8 .... **105**

JAMES THOMSEN, II: NARRATIVE UPDATE (2017) 105

A PERSONAL NOTE 113

RESOURCES 114

IMAGES OF SLAVERY **118**

FROM AFRICA TO AMERICA 118

UPCOMING WORKS **150**

Preface

A few years ago, my friend, Marita Haynes, conceived of an idea for a book that told the story of an enslaved family's experience on a Southern plantation, and their escape from bondage, aided by coded pictorial messages in strategically placed quilts. Marita passed away in 2017 before she was able to write this story and, a few months later, her husband, artist Richard Haynes, contacted me with a request to help him bring to life Marita's dream; I was honored to write this story based on Marita's vision. I consider her a co-author in this effort as the idea for this story originated with her; indeed, fidelity to her intent and vision was first and foremost in my mind as I felt her presence as though looking over my shoulder every step of the way.

Whispering Quilts is a work of fiction; however, most of the experiences of the main characters are rooted in historical facts based on firsthand accounts of former slaves, as recorded in the *Slave Narratives** and other historical sources. Additionally, many abolitionists and places mentioned in connection with the

---

* These are typewritten records prepared by the Federal Writers' Project (1936-1938), assembled by the Library of Congress. The entire collection is available at: https://www.loc.gov/collections/slave-narratives-from-the-federal-writers-project-1936-to-1938/about-this-collection

Underground Railroad are historically accurate. I have seen this blending fact and fiction described as "faction".

Whispering Quilts is the story of a young Dahomean girl who was sold or traded into slavery on the West African Slave Coast in the late 18th century, brought to America, and resold to a South Carolinian rice planter. The young girl is renamed Charlotte and forced to become a breeder, eventually dying in childbirth. Half a century later, after witnessing the savage flogging and slow murder of a runaway slave whose attempt at escape was unsuccessful, Charlotte's progeny attempt to escape the brutality of slavery to freedom in Canada with the help of White abolitionists and free Blacks. Failure is not an option. Their lives depend on reading and interpreting coded messages hidden in patterns stitched into quilts. The mystery of the young African girl's identity is not revealed until the 21st century.

The main inspiration for the fictional characters in the story came from artist Richard Haynes' own slave ancestors whose names are reflected in the story. Mr. Haynes' modern interpretation of the quilts illustrate the story, and he is represented by the James II character, who builds on the ex-slave Thomas's narrative account of his 1849 -1850 experiences as a fugitive seeking freedom with his family in Canada.

Through the modern magic of DNA testing, we know that Richard's story began in Benin, which, until the last century, was the Kingdom of Dahomey. As he noted, reflectively, "I now know where I came from, and that at least one of my enslaved forebears was born in freedom in Benin!"

Ruth M. Tappin, Ph.D.

Foreword

I confess that I have a passion for quilts and a love of history. Thus, when I was afforded the honor of reading *Whispering Quilts,* I welcomed the opportunity to learn more about the role that quilts played in facilitating the escape of slaves from bondage to freedom in Canada, and what it must have been like for these fugitives to embark on such a perilous journey. While there is disagreement about the use of quilts by abolitionists as a means of conveying coded messages to fleeing slaves, what is not in dispute is the role that abolitionists played in aiding slaves in their pursuit of freedom.

The story of the Whispering Quilts is a blend of facts and fiction (also known as "faction") and is narrated in the unpretentious voice of Thomas, the middle son of an enslaved family that attempts to escape from bondage in South Carolina to freedom in Canada, which the slaves referred to as Canaan Land. The 88-year-old Thomas recounts the harrowing ordeals he and his fugitive family suffered in their pursuit of freedom when he was about 14 years old. Guided by coded messages in ten quilt patterns, the family is aided by enslaved and free Blacks, and white abolitionists who were station masters along the Underground Railroad.

Although this is primarily a work of fiction, many places and characters in the story are based on historical and biographical facts. For example, one of the artist's (i.e., Richard Haynes) ancestors was from the Kingdom of Dahomey, which is today Benin. Underground Railroad stations such as the home of abolitionist Moses Cartland of Lee, New Hampshire, and the Rokeby place, in Ferrisburg, Vermont, were safe harbors for fugitive slaves. Additionally, it was particularly enlightening to learn about the Elgin Settlement in North Buxton, Canada, and the successful school integration of black and white students in the mid-to-late1800s at that settlement. The settlement, also known as Buxton, exists today.

Perhaps, we humans just choose to forget that which is too painful to remember; but, as I read, I realized that like so many others my knowledge of the history of slavery in the United States was superficial. Indeed, it was tempered and bounded by my limited understanding of the institution of slavery and what it must have been like to live the life of a slave; reading this story gave me a clear insight into just how deep are the wounds of this "peculiar institution." I assure you, reader, that the types of everyday circumstances and forms of punishment described in the book are based on well-documented writings contemporary to the slave period as well as historical documents such as the 1936-1938 Slave Narrative Project.

Learning about the names and places associated with the Underground Railroad, and getting glimpses into the personalities of the abolitionists, was intellectually enlightening. It certainly piqued my interest to expand my limited understanding of the technical and logistical challenges faced by abolitionists and fugitive slaves. I feel as if this book has stirred within me a desire to investigate more deeply the good, the bad, and the ugly of our country's past.

Whispering Quilts is a must-read story suitable for older children and adults. It is an easy-to-read but profound work that masterfully illustrates the dreadful condition of slavery and the inspiring efforts of the brave men and women who formed what we know to be the Underground Railroad system that guided those in bondage to freedom. It tells, too, a tale of ingeniously coded messages whispered in the patterns of handmade quilts. Valerie L. Mills, Ph.D.

Introduction

Lacking a formal mode of communication, in the planning and execution of their escape from their bondage, Africans enslaved in America developed symbols and codes to communicate with each other. Reputedly, some of these ways of communication were embedded in Negro spirituals that alerted slaves to prepare for their escape, or in quilt patterns that provided direction and guidance in their journey to freedom; however, some historians dispute the use of such symbols and codes in this manner. What is indisputable, though, is that an intricate system known as the *Underground Railroad* existed throughout the slave-holding and Free States to assist the fleeing slaves in their journey from bondage to freedom.

Running the "railroad" system was a vast network of whites of conscience who were willing to break the law and put themselves at personal risk to help fugitive slaves, as well as resist the institution of slavery. The ingenuity, courage, and endurance it took for the enslaved to initiate his or her escape are matched only by the sense of moral obligation, higher purpose, dedication, and the commitment of white abolitionists and other freed slaves to assist the fugitives in their flight to freedom.

This harrowing but hope-filled story of the *Whispering Quilts* is rooted in actual events. It could have been the experience of any one of the millions of Africans forced into slavery, who attempted the dangerous escape and journey from the Southern slave plantations of America to seek freedom in Canada.

The focus of this story is on the descendants of a young African girl from the Kingdom of Dahomey, which today is Benin; she was sold to European slavers in the 1700s. The story spans the generation of descendants from the young girl and concludes with a narrative written in 2017 by James Thomsen II, also a descendant of the enslaved girl.

Chapter 1
Thomas' Story

My name is Thomas Thomsen and, at the time of this writing, I am 88 years old. I was born in 1836, and I am the middle son of three children born into slavery on the Thomsen Plantation in Charleston, South Carolina; my father and mother were also birthed into enslavement on that same plantation. My father, James, was born in 1815, and my mother was born two years later in 1817.

Mother's name was Christine, but from a young child, everybody called her "Chrissy." My brother, Homer, was the oldest son, and he was born in 1834. Isaac, the youngest, entered this world in 1840. They are all gone now, and I alone remain to tell what I know of our family history, and what I remember about our escape from slavery to freedom—before the good Lord calls me home.

This is my written account of my family's escape from slavery in Charleston County, South Carolina in 1849, to freedom in Canada in 1850. I am writing this in my home in Mississauga, Canada, in the year 1924, and I hope that this family story will be passed down from my children and grandchildren to future generations.

The Ancestors

What I know of my family's story begins on the Atlantic Coast of West Africa where, around June or July in 1800, a young African girl was traded by other Africans in exchange for guns and other supplies. That young girl was destined to become my grandmother, Charlotte. Old Master Thomsen purchased Grandma Charlotte, who was my mother's mother, at auction in Charleston a few days after the slave ship docked there, in South Carolina. Master's wife gave her that name, Charlotte, and we never knew what her African name was.

My Mother's Mother: Grandmother Charlotte

What I know about Grandmother Charlotte, is this: She was the only one in the line of our ancestors that we could trace directly from a place and year in her journey from West Africa to America. She was about 15 years old when she arrived in Charleston Harbor on the *Forbes*, a slave ship commanded by Captain Elijah Belcher of Braintree, Massachusetts.

The young girl was placed on the auction block in Charleston, just a few days after she and the surviving slaves arrived in South Carolina. That was in September 1800. I know because a few years ago a member of the Thomsen family shared with me some of the records that the family had kept throughout slavery, which remained in their possession to present time.

Old Master Thomsen who bought Grandmother Charlotte owned one of the biggest plantations in Charleston County on account of the 600[1] slaves that he owned, and the size of his family's estate, which was over 700 acres. The estate was in St. Andrew's Parish and was located on the Ashley River in West Ashley[2]. He made his fortunes mainly in the cultivation and sale

---

[1] Plantation size was generally determined based on number of slaves owned.
[2] The fictional Thomsen Plantation in this story is based on the Drayton Hall

of rice and the breeding of slaves; however, cotton and indigo were other sources of income for the Thomsen Plantation. What I learned much later in my life is that slaves represented more than 80% of the slave masters' wealth.

Master Thomsen only bought West Africans as they were best suited for working the marshy lands of South Carolina, which was similar to the soil and climate of West Africa, and these peoples already knew how to cultivate rice. Old Master Thomsen also owned one of the grandest of the big houses in the area and, unlike many plantation owners, was not an absentee owner, but lived on the estate. Mistress Thomsen loved having lots of company, and there were many parties and gatherings held at the big house.

Grandmother Charlotte was supposed to work in the rice fields with the other enslaved peoples that Master Thomsen bought from the cargo of 1800, but he decided my grandma would be a breeder because she was built for that purpose. She was young and healthy; she had wide hips, and she had good bones and strong teeth. I don't know how such a young thing survived the

---

Plantation, similarly located on the Ashley River in West Ashley. The primary crops of the Drayton Hall Plantation were cotton, rice, and phosphate.

journey from the Slave Coast of Africa to Charleston, but all in all, she arrived in good enough form.

Breeders were very valuable to planters like Master Thomsen because they could get 15, 20 or more slave children from one good breeder—and when those babies were old enough to be put to the plough at age 14 or so, they commanded a good price on the auction block. Slave breeding and selling are what accounted for a considerable portion of Master Thomsen's wealth—and he was very wealthy indeed!

From what my mother told us, Grandma Charlotte was a fighter and did not want to be a breeder, even though life for these slaves was easier than that of a field-hand. Grandma Charlotte used to fight and scream and kick and bite. She would yell "*Ahosi! Mino!*"[3] and no amount of flogging or cutting[3] could tame her fighting nature. My mother thought that *Ahosi* and *Mino* were the African names of her mother, but she could not be sure.

In her 13 years of enslavement, Grandmother Charlotte had 12 children; some of them died, and others were sold. She must have been around 29 years old when she died in 1817 giving birth to

---

[3] Many plantation owners believed that the Negroes did not have skin, but hides, and it was only when cut that they responded to pain, which was an integral part of discipline and punishment.

her last child, who was my mother. All of Grandmother Charlotte's babies were raised by various mammies because she refused to have anything to do with the poor things when they were born. That was probably because she did not want to be forced into pregnancy by their daddy (or daddies) in the first place.

My Mother's Father: an Unknown Granddaddy

My mother's father was already living on the plantation when Old Master Thomsen brought my Grandma Charlotte there. I was told that my granddaddy was a stock slave; there were about three or four of them on the Thomsen Plantation. Their job was to impregnate the breeders[4]. I imagine that the stock slave who impregnated Grandma Charlotte must've fathered hundreds of slave babies in his lifetime; it was just a job to him. That means that my mother must have had hundreds of brothers and sisters that she never knew! *Well, now!* That is indeed something to ponder on. So, you see, that is why my mother never knew who her daddy was, and that is why we never knew his name; he could have been any of Master Thomsen's stock slaves.

---

[4] All of the descriptions of the slave experience in this story—from punishments meted out to slaves, their living and social conditions, behaviors and practices of the slaves and slave masters, as well as folk practices—are based on first-hand accounts reported by freed slaves in the Slave Narratives Project: South Carolina, Vols. 1-4, https://www.loc.gov/item/mesn141/

My Father's Daddy: Granddaddy Isaac

My father's daddy's name was Isaac. Granddaddy Isaac was hung on the big oak tree at the back of the big house of the Thomsen Plantation a few months after my father James was born. The old mammy who raised my father told him that they killed his Daddy Isaac because he had the run-away blood in him. He just kept trying to get to freedom and kept getting caught. Neither whipping, nor branding, nor the stock, nor other types of tortures ever cured Granddaddy Isaac of the run-away fever.

In those days, some slave masters thought it better, in the end, to kill these kinds of trouble-making slaves because they could infect other slaves with that run-away fever. Public punishment and executions of recaptured slaves were further means of control meant to instill fear and deter others from attempting to flee from their bondage. When they killed Granddaddy Isaac in a most brutal manner, it was a public execution. I guess my father might have inherited some of that run-away fever from his Daddy, Isaac.

Old Mammy

Since my daddy's mother died when he was young, he was raised by a mammy, but nursed by any one of the breeders who had enough breast-milk to spare. In those days the old women on Master Thomsen's plantation took care of the slave babies and very young children when the mothers died, or when they did not want to suckle their babies—like Grandmother Charlotte. The mammies also took care of the babies when the women had to go back to work in the fields after childbirth. Generally, these mammies used to be breeders themselves. But it wasn't like that on every plantation.

On some plantations, the mothers had to tie their babies to their backs and work in the fields like that. When the babies grew too old to carry on their backs anymore, they would secure the babies to a tree close by the rows. Sometimes babies got bit by the red ants and died; sometimes they got bit by snakes, or else died from the heat of the sun or lack of water.

My mother said that some planters used to have their field-hands make a big trough, and there the mothers put the babies while they worked. One day, on one of the plantations that used this method, the rains came suddenly when the field-hands were way down the rows, far away from the babies. The mothers ran down the rows to get to their babies, but it rained so hard that by the time they got to them the rains had near filled up the trough and drowned all of them.

My mother said she heard tell that the wailings and carrying-on of those poor mothers went on for days, and they got thrashed for the ruckus they caused, too! Although Old Master Thomsen was a hard master and quick with the whip, he was not a foolish one. He knew the value of a healthy child for he grew wealthy and prosperous through the cultivation and sale of healthy slaves.

My father's mammy told him that my grandfather, Isaac, kept running away because he was running from pain and sorrow. You see, his wife, my father's mother, died around the time my daddy was born. My father's mammy said that my father loved that woman more than his own life; however, she would not tell my daddy his mother's name, or how his mother died. Nobody would speak my mother's name.

Whenever my daddy pestered the old mammy with questions, she would shake her head in sorrow and say to him: "Lordy, lordy chile! Quiet, now! *Jest let sleepin' dogs lie!*" Sometimes she would say "*Don't' trouble Trouble, lessen Trouble trouble you!*" So, I have no history on my father's mother—but whatever happened to her must have been pretty awful because it seemed that it was enough to terrify those who knew about it so that they were too scared to even think on it, much less talk about it!

Everyone knows that many of the plantation owners had a boundless capacity to commit inhumane acts of depravity upon their slaves. *Yessir.* To have the power of life or death over another human being can bring out the devil in a Christian! That is what my mother used to say.

Chapter 2

Marriage and Family

My father's name was James, and he was two years older than my mother, Christine; everybody called my mother, *Chrissy*. These two motherless and fatherless children grew up together and were raised by the same old mammy and nursed at the breasts of breeders. They played together as children, fell in love, and jumped the broom when my mother was 17 years old. That was round about 1833.

Some of the kindlier planters allowed their slaves to marry in this way, but that didn't mean anything at all because the masters could sell you, your wife, or your children whenever they had a mind to. So, jumping the broom was a kind of marriage that gave comfort to slaves in love, but it had no recognition under the law. However, many slave owners knew that they benefited from this broom-jumping ceremony because the children born of this marriage belonged to the master, and the family units formed from the unions were powerful glues that kept the slaves from running away. When my parents jumped the broom[5], us children came pretty fast after that!

First came Homer; he was born in 1834. I was born in 1836, and Isaac was born in 1840. But in between Homer and me, my mother lost a child, and between Isaac and me, she miscarried another. Yes, my parents, my two brothers, and I were born into slavery on the Thomsen Plantation in South Carolina.

Of all of us, only Grandmother Charlotte was born in freedom because she was born in Africa. But when our parents and us boys took our first breaths, we were all born into bondage and were the property of Old Master Thomsen right there and then. When Old Master Thomsen passed on, we became the property of his oldest son, young Master Anthony Thomsen. And he was just as hard and shrewd as his daddy, and quick with the whip, too!

---

[5] Jumping the broom was a practice that originated in Ghana. For more information on this African practice, see
https://aaregistry.org/story/jumping-the-broom-a-short-history/

Home, Not-so-sweet Home Life

My parents and us boys lived in a small one-room hut made of rough-cut wood that had daub[6] between the slats to keep out the weather. Our shelter was raised off the ground and had a wooden floor; the roof was made from shingles that sometimes leaked and often, like the other slaves, my daddy would put palmetto leaves over it until he got the time to patch up those leaks.

My father made a bed from two sturdy planks that he and my mother slept on, and these doubled as benches when not in use for sleeping on. He also made a skinny table that was the length of their plank bed; this we pulled up to the plank bed to eat on when the weather was bad—otherwise, we ate our meals outside, sitting on tree stumps cut to size of a stool, and on the wooden step of our hut. When not in use, the table was pushed up against the wall and served as Homer's bed at night. There was no other furniture in the space as just those two pieces occupied too much space in that little hut.

Isaac and I slept on the floor on one big bed made from old rags and straw; this material was stuffed into a sack made with a couple old blankets to form a mattress. Every three years or so

---

[6] A mixture of mud, twigs, and straw or grass

Master Thomsen and the Mistress gave us slaves a new blanket, and the old ones were put to various uses such as patching up the worn-out mattress covers. We had to discard the stuffing quite frequently, and every morning we pushed the rough mattress under our parents' plank beds before we left for work. I don't think we ever got used to this rough bed because of the hardness and prickliness of the material from which the filling was made.

Our few possessions consisted of the herbs my mother gathered to dry, a couple cooking pots, the few wooden bowls and utensils made by my father, and the sparse bits of clothing we owned; these were was hung on pegs made from branches embedded in the daub, or sat on shelves made from rough-cut lumber. Of these, my mother would say that the pots and the herbs, which she hung from the ceiling to dry, were her most valuable possessions.

Just like the other cabins, we had a small hearth with a chimney that was made of tabby[7]. We used that for cooking on bad-weather days, and for keeping warm in the cold months, but probably because of a fear of starting a fire, none of the slaves were allowed to prepare meals inside the cabin on a daily basis;

---

[7] Tabby: a mixture made from crushed oyster shells and sand, dissolved in water and heated over a fire forming a type of cement

so, like the other slaves, we had a fire pit outside, where we cooked our one-pot meals. All of the slave huts were similar in construction and size; however, the ones that my parents' forebears lived in were not like the ones I knew when I lived on the plantation.

Back in Grandmother Charlotte's day, and in the 17th and 18 centuries, the slave dwellings were more like those in West Africa. Those early dwellings had walls made of wattle and daub[8], and the roofs were thatched with palmetto fronds or suchlike. The floors were of dirt, and they slept right on that earthen ground. Since they were not raised off the ground, the floors got muddy when it rained, and these huts fell to termites and rot quite often, so the slaves had to rebuild them every few years. Then, in the 1800s, the abolitionists started making a ruckus about slave treatment and living conditions, so some of the plantation owners began making huts like the ones my brothers and I lived in, with wooden floors raised off the ground.

I heard that right up to the Civil War some plantations still used the crude types of dwelling from Grandmother Charlotte's time

---

[8] Wattle: twigs and branches woven into sections that comprised the walls of the hut, and fastened to poles in the ground. Grasses and twigs were mixed with clay and daubed unto these structures to complete them. Subsequent daubing thickened the walls and made them sturdier.

because it was cheaper than the wood dwellings. You see, many planters did not have a mind to waste money on the slaves' comfort as every cent spent in time or treasure reduced their profits by that amount.

The early slaves brought with them the memory and skills of their West African culture, in this way, they influenced slave architecture, agriculture, cooking, pottery-making, and lots of other skills that benefitted and enriched the plantation owners. Nevertheless, how much more miserable it must have been for slaves before and during Grandmother Charlotte's early days that it was for us! And, believe me—life was very miserable for us, even though we had it easier than the field slaves!

Family Meals

Rice was what we mainly ate, and corn followed as a close second. We had a small garden in which we grew collard greens, okra, sweet potatoes and a few other vegetables. South Carolina is in the area of the United States called the Low Country[9]. The climate and land in the Low Country area are just like West Africa, where my Grandmother Charlotte came from, and that is how those planters came to plant crops like rice and sugarcane in those areas. It is the slaves who brought that knowledge to the New World; the plantation owners did not know a thing about cultivating rice.

Since the Thomsen Plantation was on the coast, we also had access to fish and crabs because of the sea and the marshes—and we all helped each other best we could. We got no meat except some of the meanest parts of the animal every now and then, but especially at Christmas; these were the head, ribs, feet, or entrails of the animal—however, we did get pork fat for cooking. That was a good eating day when we had some seafood or meat! Everything we cooked was all cooked together; this is now called a one-pot meal.

---

[9] The Low Country included the Carolinas, Georgia, and parts of Florida.

Our clothes were no better than our meals. We got a rough set of clothes once a year—but no coat. Those clothes had to last the entire year and, like the rest of the slave women, we were given raw cloth, which was spun on the plantation and our mothers had to make our summer clothes from that. My mother learned weaving and sewing skills from the breeders whose tasks these were. My brothers and I had britches, but at some plantations, the children only had a tunic and never got britches until they were old enough for the plough. At a very tender age, we were given chores that increased as we got older.

Many slave owners beat the children for small or large infractions or when they didn't do their chores well, but Master Thomsen didn't allow for beating his young slaves until they were at least seven years old. Every child I knew, including my brothers and me, got the switch or the paddle a few times. Master Thomsen thought it prudent to switch us so that we would get to know pain as an incentive to work harder and to keep us in line. Almost every slave child was witness to brutality in some form or another and learned and understood from an early age how to be submissive to the authority of white men, women, and even white children; consequently, they learned early the art of putting on Massa.

Puttin' on Massa

When I was a child of 4 or 5 years old, one of my first chores was to lie down under the feet of Old Master Thomsen to soak up his arthritis, aches, and pains into my body. Under my parents' instruction, and from observation, like the other slave children chosen for this purpose, I learned to "put on Massa" by pretending that, indeed, all of his ailments were transferred from his old arthritic body to mine.

While under the feet of Old Master Thomsen, I would squirm and groan and twist my body into impressive contortions that convinced the old man that his discomforts were being lessened by this ridiculous ritual. My reward for soaking up all of these infirmities ranged from a piece of candy to bread with jam, or suchlike.

It was in the Master's best interest to keep us young ones healthy and strong for the powers of absorption to work! There were many other ways to put on Massa, and these tactics were often credited for saving a house slave from a whipping, or other punishment.

Work Life for Daddy James

My father was a gifted carpenter and an excellent painter. Today he would be put in the category of a skilled artisan. He could build anything Master Thomsen or the Mistress called for and mostly worked making whatever they needed. He took care of much of the repairs on the estate, so he did not work in the fields because they valued his skills so highly. My father also helped repair the roofs on the slave huts when they leaked, so he was well-loved and respected among the slaves. He enjoyed decorating the furniture and various objects that the Thomsens called for and gained their favor, so he was treated well.

We heard tell that on many occasions Master Thomsen refused purchase offers for my father by other envious planters, even though their offers were generous. Nevertheless, he never forgot the thrashing he got from a new overseer who did not know that my father was not a field-hand. When he saw my father leaning against a tree, taking a little rest from helping move one of his heavy pieces that he created to Master Thomsen's dressing room, that overseer thought my father was being lazy and was shirking his duties by not being in the fields.

That overseer was brutal and quick with the whip. He tied my daddy over a fat tree trunk that was kept for that purpose and proceeded to thrash him. He only stopped when Master Thomsen came hollering at him from the big house, all red in the face. One of the other slaves had run up to the big house yelling that the overseer was nigh to killing my father. By the time Master Thomsen got to them, my father was cut and bloodied.

When Master Thomsen got wind of what happened he was madder than a hornet; he did not mind so much if my father had gotten the whipping because he deserved it, but Master Thomsen was very concerned that my father would not be able to complete the other building projects that he was working on. Master Thomsen made a pretty penny taking orders on furniture, which my father and the other wood-workers and apprentices built; of course, the fruits of my father's labor belonged to Master Thomsen. After the whipping, my daddy got a week off to heal; yes, my mother's poultices[10] and herbs helped him in his healing.

Daddy James taught us carpentry at an early age, and that is how my brother Homer and I were able to stay out of the fields, and even though he was the youngest, Isaac was also showing a talent

---

[10] Slaves brought to the New World knowledge of herbs and their properties; poultices were made by combining two or more herbs into a paste, which was applied topically to wounds or infected parts of the body.

for the craft. My father never took for granted the relative freedom that he felt in being exempt from the fields, and he warned us continually to be diligent and to work as hard and as well as we could. Those skills were to serve us well in Canada, which my mother called *Canaan Land*.

Work Life for Mother Chrissy

My mother worked in the big house from the time she was a young child. The breeders taught her to spin and weave at a very early age and she was quick with the needle, too. That was one reason she got to work in the big house. When she was not doing those tasks, she was helping to cook the meals, clean the house, scrub the floors, beat the carpets, attend to the Thomsen children, and whatever else needed doing.

My mother told us that at first she lived in the big house and slept on a plank in a corner in the kitchen. She had to be ready to respond immediately if the mistress or any other member of the household called for her. Although the work never seemed to end, she had enough food to eat, and like most house-servants, she had more than one set of clothing because the mistress sometimes gave her and the other house servants the young mistresses' hand-me-downs. Plantation mistresses took pride in having clean house-servants.

My mother said that something happened and when she was 13 years old the mistress no longer let her sleep at the big house, although she still had to do all the chores, same as before. Instead, she was sent to live in a cabin with an old mammy, where she slept on the floor with several other children. She had to get up with the field-hands when the overseer blew the horn to wake up the slaves and had to go up to the big house while it was still dark to start work.

My mother worked as long as the field hands did, and didn't get to go back to her cabin until long after nightfall. She used to be terrified that a haint[11] would grab her because she had to pass by the big oak tree behind the kitchen where slaves were routinely tied and beaten. Like many other slaves, she believed that tree held the pain of those souls who died there, under the lash.

During that time, and up until she married my father, the Mistress seemed to hold a particular hatred toward my mother and found many opportunities to punish her terribly. She whipped her on many occasions for any and no reason. But my father loved my mother since they were children in Old Mammy's care. When she was sixteen, my daddy mustered up the courage to ask Master if he could jump the broom with Chrissy; it was the year 1833. To his great joy, Master Thomsen agreed. It seemed that the mistress eased up on my mother after the jumping of the broom. Years later, when we were on the run to

---

[11] Haints: restless earth-bound spirits of the dead.

Canada, my mother finally told us boys what happened to make the Mistress hate her so much.

My Mother's Secrets

Mother had two secrets that would have resulted in severe punishment if Master Thomsen were to find out about them. While she was yet very young, my mother developed an interest in medicinal herbs and grew up to be considered a "yarb[12]" healer. Young children were always catching the worms, and my mother would boil up a pot of yarb to worm us and other slave kids. That was the worst tasting drink you could imagine, but it sure took care of those worms!

My mother knew how to make poultices to draw out infections from sores, and to heal the wounds from whippings, too. She learned all of this herb medicine from Old Mammy. The slaves' ancestors brought that knowledge from Africa and also learned a great deal from the native Indians, which they passed on to other generations of slaves.

In those days the plantation owners didn't allow for slaves to practice slave medicine because they were afraid that the slaves knew about making poisons, which they could use to kill the masters and their household, so the yarb doctors were very secretive about what they knew about herbs and healing. Every

---

[12] "Yarb" is a colloquial term for "herb"

once in a while, slaves whispered about a master or his family being poisoned by his most trusted slaves.

One time there was a big ruckus about a young slave girl named Maggie who baked a cake with leaves from the oleander shrub and fed it to her young charge[13], who was the Master's favorite child. That slave said that the child was wicked and enjoyed making up stories that caused her to get unjust whippings. She only intended for the child to get sick; however, the child died. Maggie was flogged brutally and then hanged. My mother seemed to have a natural talent for herb medicine and other slaves called on her for her special poultices—especially after whippings—so they kept her doctoring secrets safe. It was not until much later that she told me what stirred this particular interest in herbs.

The second secret was that mother could read and write. This was a secret that only my father, my brothers, and I knew. It was against the law for slaves to read and write, punishable by death. Mistress Haverhill, the Master's sister-in-law, lived with the Thomsens after the death of her husband.

---

[13] This account is based on the folklore story of Chloe, a house servant who poisoned her young charge in like manner.

In his will, Mistress Haverhill's husband left his plantation to his wife but made his brother the administrator of the estate. She was the daughter of a Methodist minister from one of the Northern states. From the time that she moved to the South after her marriage, throughout all the years that she lived—first—on her husband's estate, then in her brother-in-law's home, she secretly held abolitionist sentiments.

Mistress Haverhill had learned very early to keep those sentiments hidden; however, she found ways to rebel against the slave system and keep her peace with God: she devised ways to teach the brightest slaves to read, write, and count. Over the years, little by little, those slaves disappeared, never to be seen again.

Mistress Thomsen had allowed my mother to be Mistress Haverhill's personal maid and this station allowed them to spend a lot of time together, with no supervision; it was during these times that she taught my mother to read. My mother was one of her most astute students and absorbed everything Mistress Haverhill poured into her young mind like a sponge.

One of the most important things that Miss Haverhill taught my mother was the art of "speaking proper" but only to do so privately during their secret lessons and to speak in regular slave dialect when around other slaves or in the presence of any white person. This was another way of *puttin' on Massa*. Miss Haverhill also impressed on my mother to never, ever let any slave know that she knew how to read, write, and "speak proper" because it was common that some slaves would gladly get other slaves in trouble to find favor with their owners.

My mother loved Miss Haverhill, and did everything she was told to do; however, once my parents jumped the broom, my mother disobeyed Miss Haverhill and taught my father reading, writing, and counting. My mother was smart and resourceful, and when she taught my father these skills, she used the back of one of the many loose floorboards of their cabin to write on, and pieces of charcoal as a writing tool. She was always careful to write lightly, and use sand to scour off the writing on the board.

When us boys came along, mother also taught us these skills when we were old enough to understand the connection between Master's anger and punishments such as whippings, hangings, torture. Slave children learned very early the harsh realities of surviving on a plantation—especially when a member of their family was the one being punished.

A Brutal Punishment

One hot day in August of 1849, in the middle of the week, all the field hands and all the house servants and other slaves were made to gather in a field that had a little hill in the middle of it. That field and the rise of the mound made it a natural gathering place where major punishments were to take place because it allowed all of the slaves gathered there to see what was going on. Sometimes the Master held special events there, and at those times he would set up prettied-up tents and a central gazebo in which guests would sit while, in the field below, slaves were made to entertain the guests by displaying feats of strength or talent.

On these festive occasions entertainment might be tying slaves together by the hand—two-by-two—blindfolding them and making them fight till exhaustion or death, or whichever came first. On these occasions, only those slaves selected to serve or entertain guests would be present at these events. The winner always got a prize, which might be food, likker[14], or both. However, whenever all of the plantation's slaves were called to gather there, which was perhaps two or three times a year, we all knew someone was going to die that day, and in a brutal manner.

---

[14] Liquor

This time, all the plantation slaves were gathered together, looking up toward the hill. There was a box just sitting there; the overseer stood next to it, with three drivers behind it. There was a sizeable upright stake buried in the ground on the other side of the box, and it had a big black iron ring with a rope hanging from it. Everyone—except perhaps the littlest children—knew that there was a slave in that box and that he would be tied so that he would hang from that big iron ring. My mother and father drew us tighter to them, and we could feel the tremor in their bodies. After a while, Master Thomsen came and ordered the box to be opened. From it, the drivers dragged a limp bundle of rags; it was Lewis, a field hand who had run away more than a month ago.

Apparently, Lewis did not get beyond the Thomsen estate because he got lost and disoriented. There was a big ruckus when the slave drivers realized that he was missing; the overseer and divers searched all of the cabins and even whipped a few slaves that they believed had information about Lewis.

The slave catchers went looking for him with their bloodhounds, but Lewis hid in the swamps, so they lost track of him. But the August heat and swamp sickness got to poor Lewis, and when they finally found him, he was weak and hungry. Without tools and preparation, he was not able to get too far but still managed to hold out in the swamps for almost a month; hunger had driven him back toward the plantation—perhaps in search of food. Today, Master Thomsen was going to use Lewis as an example to show what happened to runaway slaves. Master Thomsen wanted every slave—young and old—to remember this day, lest anyone harbored thoughts of running again.

What they did to poor Lewis cannot be described in this letter. They stripped him naked and tied his hands up above his head so that he hung from that iron ring. They pulled him up on that pole so that his feet were no longer touching the ground. Lewis' eyes were wild with fear, and his mouth was moving, but I don't know what he was saying. First Master Thomsen whipped poor Lewis, who twisted and writhed on that pole.

Then the drivers took turns flogging him until they could not raise the whip anymore; they stripped his naked body of its flesh. By this time I was sure that he was dead—but then they poured brine into his wounds[15] and a scream such as never came from a man before, came forth from that poor soul. The cries and wailing from those gathered there were such like you cannot

---

[15] Horrific beatings and tortures were routine during slavery; these included hanging slaves in torturous positions and leaving them to die slowly. Pouring brine, peppers, and various types of concoctions designed to inflict maximum pain and discomfort into the wounds of flogged slaves was a common practice.

imagine; they haunt me to this day! His poor old mother was in that crowd that day, and she fainted dead away.

At first, my mother tried to clamp her hands over Isaac's eyes and mine, but my father had such a look on his face that I had never seen before or since. He pulled my mother's hands away and said, hoarsely, "Let them see! They must know!" She did not even notice that he was speaking proper English. When those drivers were done with poor Lewis, they set the dogs on him[16]; what was left of him after the dogs were done was left hanging from that pole for the rest of the week. The buzzards and other wild animals finished him off.

Years later, my father told me that it was at that moment that he decided to run away to freedom with his entire family. As he witnessed the brutal murder of poor Lewis, he realized that he was looking at—not Lewis—but his own father who was also murdered for running away repeatedly. My father said then that he would *rather die on the road to freedom than live out the rest of his life on a plantation in slavery!*

That night, while we were still traumatized and terrorized by what we had witnessed, in the privacy of our hut, I heard my father

---

[16] A similar account is recalled in "Africans in America: A Slave is tortured".

whispering to my mother and what he was saying terrified me even more. I looked at Isaac, and he was asleep, but tears had streaked his face. I looked up at where Homer was lying on the long table that was his bed at night; he was staring up at the ceiling, and his profile looked like it was carved from stone. I knew that he, too, heard my father's whisperings; he and I never spoke of what we heard that night.

Chapter 3

Fear and Flight: The Planning

My parents knew there were ways for people to escape to the north because—even though some runaway slaves like poor Lewis were caught—every once in a while they heard rumors of those who were not. Every night my father and mother spoke softly about would it would take to make it to Canada, which they referred to as Canaan Land. They prayed, too. I often fell asleep to their whispered prayers as they pleaded with God to show them the way and to make a way where there seemed to be none. They encouraged each other, reminding each other that it only took the faith of a mustard seed to break through that slavery mountain to get to freedom

One Sunday, in October, my mother asked my father to go down to the creek with her to hunt for crabs. We could see that she seemed to be trying to contain excitement about something. It was there that she told him that Mistress Haverhill had been telling her how to get to Canaan Land while they were working on three Christmas quilts.

It was a custom of Mistress Haverhill to sew quilts to give as Christmas presents every year. With the help of Grandmother Chrissy, she created three identical quilts and gave one to Mistress Thomsen, one to her sister in Philadelphia, and one to her grown daughter who lived in Baltimore; these she designed and stitched in great privacy. The quilts were prized for their uniqueness and workmanship, and Mrs. Thomsen made sure that the two women were never disturbed when they worked on them. Thus, Mistress Haverhill was able to teach Grandmother Chrissy many things during these times.

And so for the next few weeks, they stitched together three sets of quilt patterns, which amounted to 30 quilt patches. Every time they sat down to sew a quilt patch, Mistress Haverhill would stare intently at my mother and say, "Now Chrissy, pay attention to what you are doing because the Good Book says *he who has ears, let him hear; and he who has eyes, let him see!* I don't want you messing up these patterns!" And my mother would say smartly, "Yes, Ma'am!" because those words were a signal that her mistress used when alerting her that she was about to teach or share something significant with my mother.

Well, that Mistress Haverhill was a clever woman! Every year, in August, she visited her folks in Philadelphia for one month; turns out that that year, after poor Lewis' murder, she had quietly taken up with the abolitionist Quakers, who had devised secret codes to help slaves escape to freedom. These codes were patterns on quilt patches[17]; as they cut out and sewed together each pattern, Mrs. Haverhill told my mother what they represented.

"Chrissy," she said to my mother, "today we will sew the North Star pattern. Did you know that when sailors followed the North Star, it led them straight to where they were going? " Then she explained to my mother how to locate the Little Dipper and the North Star in the Southern sky at night.

Another time she said, "Chrissy, today we will work on the *Flying Geese* pattern. Did you know where all those flying geese are headed from when they fly over this plantation in the fall?"

"No, Ma'am."

"North, Chrissy, *north!* Straight north to Canada; that is why they are called 'Canada geese', you know! In February and March,

---

[17] The use of quilt patterns to encode messages is disputed and regarded as romanticized myth in many scholarly circles.

when they stretch their long necks and fly in that V formation, that means the season is changing, and it is time to go home. They all rise up like the Hebrews rose up out of slavery, and they fly away to the Promised Land!" Mistress Haverhill explained that the North Star was that big star at the top of the handle of the cluster of stars that looked like a little dipper, or a plough. My mother said Mistress Haverhill looked hard at her when she spoke of these things, making sure that she was paying attention.

First, Mistress Haverhill told my mother Chrissy the story of the quilt patterns; next, she made my mother repeat the story as they worked on each subsequent set. By the time they completed the 30 quilt patches, Mother knew what each pattern represented. Now they all had to be stitched together into three quilts so that each quilt had 10 pieces; that task would take them right up to the end of November.

During that time, Mistress Haverhill had more to tell my mother. "By now you know that the quilt patches tell a story, Chrissy," she said. "That story can help you get safely to freedom. Many people are working hard to set your people free and most of the people they help go straight to Canada, where there is no slavery. I believe that you and James and your boys can have a good Christian life in Canada. God has prepared you for that!"

And so for the next few weeks, as they stitched together the three quilts, Mistress Haverhill explained that there was a network of good Christians between South Carolina and Canada who helped guide slaves north to freedom and this network was called an "Underground Railroad." She told my mother Chrissy what it was; who started it[18], and how it worked. She described how messages were transmitted to slaves hoping to run away through spirituals, as well as through the quilt patches. She explained what to do when she heard certain spirituals, and how to read the front and back of the quilt patterns.

At the back of the quilts, some of the stitching had crooked lines with knotty lumps. Each stitch stood for a mile, every lump a safe-house – or a place with supplies. The darns on the back of the quilt squares showed how far away it may be from a safe-house; the slant of the stitch guided the runaway to head right or left.

Mistress Haverhill explained that good people who can be trusted hung these quilts outside a window, over fences, clotheslines, porch rails, or folded them over rocking chairs on porches; these

---

[18] The Quakers were at the forefront of efforts to assist slave in their escape efforts.

were common practices employed to dry or air-out quilts, blankets, or rugs and carpets, and attracted no attention whatsoever.

I remember the night when Father and Mother told us we would be leaving the plantation; they did not have to warn us to keep this information secret as Lewis' death was still fresh in our minds—nevertheless, they did. They calmed our fright and panic by assuring us that Lewis did not have people to help him, but many people were waiting to help us, and we would be better prepared than poor Lewis.

Mother said the journey would be long and hard and dangerous. I can still see the fire in my mother's eyes as she clenched her hand into a fist and repeated, fiercely, what my father said the night of poor Lewis' murder by the Master and his men: "*I would rather that we died on the road to freedom than live out our lives on a plantation in slavery!*" I was just a young lad of 13 or 14 when my parents decided to escape slavery with my two brothers and me[19].

---

[19] Eighty-nine percent of runaway slaves were male, and 76 percent were younger 35 years of age. The percentage of fugitives fleeing as a family unit was extremely low.

The Monkey Wrench

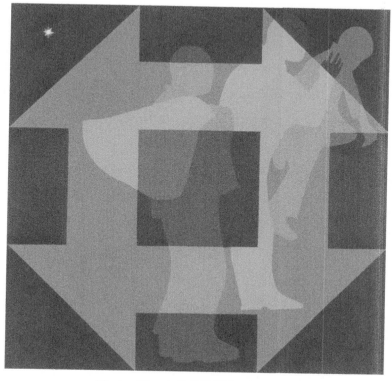

Monkey Wrench © 2018 Richard Haynes
NOTE: All full color quilt paintings may be viewed at:
http://artistrichardhaynes.com/undergroundrailroad.html

By The River Jordan: The Monkey Wrench Quilt

Then, one Sunday in late November 1849, as mother was preparing food, she heard a soft whistling nearby and without thinking she started humming the tune as she stirred the pot. Suddenly, she straightened right up from leaning over that pot of okra, rice, greens, and fish and looked around. She remembered what Mistress Haverhill said about messages in songs—and it suddenly came to mind how Mistress Haverhill looked at her when she said one day, out of the blue, "Moses led the Hebrews out of Egypt to Canaan Land…"

Mother caught sight of the whistler as he paused briefly between two cabins down the ways from our own—it was Old Egypt who lived down at the bottom of the rows of slave huts, close to the edge of the woods, next to the creek where he caught crabs for the big house. Barely glancing at her, he sang softly *"I looked over Jordan, and whut did I see…coming fo' to carry me home!"*

In shock, my mother realized that Old Egypt aided Mistress Haverhill in helping slaves escape from the Thomsen plantation. In fact, it was he who helped to identify to Mistress Haverhill which slaves would be most likely to make it safely to Canaan land. We couldn't believe that this old slave who shuffled among us every day actually helped slaves to run away!

Old Egypt was named after that part of the world from which his parents came. He lived alone in his cabin with his wife, Fara. Fara got her name as a joke because of the story of the pharaohs from Egypt, and since her husband's name was Egypt, she became Fara, which was a corruption of "pharaoh"; everybody called the old couple "Uncle" and "Aunty".

Apart from being responsible for catching crabs, fish, and other seafood, Uncle Egypt seemed to be a Jack-of-all-trades; he took care of the stables and fixed the wagon wheels and such, and his wife did much of the washing and weaving. Fara lived in the big house during the week but was allowed to stay at the cabin from Saturday night to Sunday night. They were among the few slaves on the plantation that Master Thomsen trusted most.

My mother said her heart near jumped out of her chest; it was the signal to go down to the "River Jordan", which was the creek down below the slave quarters. If there were a message for her, there would be a quilt hanging somewhere down there; wherever it was, that is where the code in the quilt pattern would be waiting to speak to her.

My mother called my father and told him they needed to draw some water, and he must go down to the creek with her. Sundays were the only days of rest for the slaves, and it was not unusual for slave families to do tasks together, or engage with others in the slave quarters. My father started to argue, but the look on my mother's face told him that he just better do as she said.

Sure enough, when they got to the creek, there was a quilt hanging from the clothesline in Uncle Egypt's yard—it was the *Monkey Wrench* quilt! The message of the quilt piece was that we needed ways to prepare for survival during our escape attempt. We might need to catch rabbits and other small game, and even protect the family from wild animals or man, if need be; this was the signal to start gathering food and tools.

My daddy said that he felt as if his heart would thump right out of his chest. He determined right there and then to keep his eyes and ears open, and trust my mother's instincts, so at the end of every day's work, no matter how late at night it was, my father went down to the creek for water and kept an eye out for the next message. They knew that the next message would be one that instructed them to set out on the journey right away.

The Wagon Wheel

The Wagon Wheel © 2018 Richard Haynes
NOTE: All full color quilt paintings may be viewed at:
http://artistrichardhaynes.com/undergroundrailroad.html

The Wagon Wheel Quilt

About two or three weeks later, about the middle of December on the Lord's Day, my parents were working in the vegetable garden. Suddenly they heard the voice of the same man singing softly:

> *Go down Moses*
> *Way down in Egypt land*
> *Tell ole Pharaoh to*
> *Let my people go!*

My mother knew immediately what she had to do. My mother plucked some okra and greens and headed down to Old Egypt's land with the provisions folded in her apron. When she got there, sure enough, hanging from the clothesline, was a quilt with the *Wagon Wheel* and the *Flying Geese* patterns patched right into the middle of it.

Old Egypt and Fara were one of the few slaves to own a quilt blanket, which his wife patched together from old scraps of cloth given to her by the Mistress on account of the fact that Fara was one of the best weavers and seamstresses on the plantation. Old Egypt was sitting on a tree trunk that was cut off at the right height for sitting—chewing and puffing on his corn-cob pipe, while Miss Fara was sweeping the yard with a broom made of twigs. Well, my mother and Aunty Fara got to talking about the

49

okra harvest and admiring the quilt, all the while examining the stitching closely.

The back of the Wagon Wheel patch had a line of 50 stitches between two lumps of the thread. From the message of the 50 stitches on the *Wagon Wheel* quilt, my mother knew that meant that when we left on our journey, we'd be on our own for at least 50 miles.

The Flying Geese

Flying Geese: © 2018 Richard Haynes
NOTE: All full color quilt paintings may be viewed at:
http://artistrichardhaynes.com/undergroundrailroad.html

The Flying Geese Quilt

As they chatted by the clothesline, there was a steady honking overhead. "Jest you look at dem geese," Old Egypt said. "At dis time of de yar all dem geese be heading south from Canada where they came from. Yessuh! Dey is sure in a hurry to get here from Canaan land—but come Febry, March, dey be heading norfh again, right back to Canaan Land!"

My mother picked up on the word "north" and "Canaan Land".

The geese always flew south from Canada at this time of the year, and Canada was in the opposite direction of the bird's flight. Every year, from October or so, they flew over the plantations in a V formation that signified the changing of the season, honking and straining their long necks forward. My mother looked up at the honking birds as they passed overhead.

"Do you reckon dey will all get here from dere home up north by day after Cris'mas, Uncle Egypt?" she asked. "Do you reckon dey will make it back north by March?"

Old Egypt puffed and squinted at her through a cloud of smoke. "Well," he drawled and puffed again. "Iffen dey stays pointed norfh, an' if de Good Lawd wills it, dey sure gwine get home soon enough!"

From the message in Old Egypt's observations she knew that we must soon head north, in the opposite direction of the arriving geese, and after traveling about 50 miles, we would be picked up by a wagon; we just had to be sure we were heading north. But by mentioning a specific date in her question, my mother was also telling him the time of our planned escape. My parents decided that the escape would be on the night after Christmas, which was only a couple weeks away, and they quietly listened and paid attention to the flying geese to know which way was north.

Chapter 4

The Escape

I
t was in the year 1849—more than 75 years ago—when we made our escape on Wednesday, December 26, but I remember it all like it was yesterday. We left on a drizzly, moonless night. It helped that Master Thomsen was hosting a grand party in the big house that night, as he did every night from Christmas to December 31, when the white folks welcomed in the New Year.

Christmas was a time of brief respite for us slaves, and we were not worked as hard, watched as carefully, or beaten as often. During this holiday time, on most plantations, the slaves were given extra food, a new set of clothing; they were supplied with—and expected to drink—as much whiskey as they could hold. Young Master Thomsen allowed the slaves to have their own celebrating in the big barn behind the stables and for this kindness, he was rewarded with many slave babies nine months later. We took this opportunity to scrounge up as much food as possible.

All of the free likker and the ease-up from work and whippings gave the drunken slaves a false sense of freedom, and since they were so likkered-up, there was hardly an incentive to run; *yessir,* young Master Thomsen did not worry about any of his slaves running away. I remember hearing my parents whispering about the rains at that time of the year, and worrying about how a body could catch the fever, or be slowed down in other ways.

The rains in South Carolina lasted from December to February and started up again in June through August. However, every once in a while we heard of a slave from other plantations who escaped during the Christmas holidays; but that did not happen very often. Since none of the Thomsen slaves had ever tried to run during the Christmas holidays, my parents decided that this holiday-time was the best time for us to make our escape.

On account of worrying about sickness troubles because of the rains, my mother had already collected and added to her supply a variety of herbs that she had dried for the journey to freedom. My mother knew which herbs cured the colds and fevers, killed the worms, and healed the wounds from the lashings or insect bites.

All of that day, on December 26, it was raining off and on; we prayed as we waited for the night to fall, too tense and frightened to talk much. We had mingled with the other slaves and made sure that the Master and Mistress saw us about. Then, as the evening drew close, we retreated to our cabin and stayed there, waiting and listening.

When, at last, night fell, little by little the noise of the merriment quieted down in the big barn and around the slave quarters. Soon, the flickering fires in the outside pits were reduced to barely glowing embers or had burned out or quenched by the rain entirely. My father nodded, and we stood up.

My mother reached out, and grabbed my father's hand, signaling that it was time to join hands in prayer. We each bowed our heads, and my father whispered a prayer, asking for traveling mercies, and protection from all harms and dangers seen and unseen. Then, grasping our meager possessions tightly, we slipped into the darkness, skirted the quarters and headed down toward Uncle Egypt's hut, sticking close together as we gripped each others' hand in a human chain.

The North Star

The North Star © 2018 Richard Haynes
NOTE: All full color quilt paintings may be viewed at:
http://artistrichardhaynes.com/undergroundrailroad.html

The North Star Quilt

By the time we reached Uncle Egypt's hut, we were shivering more from fear than from any effect of the weather. Hanging on the clothesline was the same quilt that my mother had admired a few days earlier—except this time there was another quilt patch right above the two that she had seen before. It was the North Star pattern. Its position above the other two pieces indicated we were to keep going straight ahead, and we must follow the North Star.

We headed into the woods and kept looking at the sky, but there was a cloud cover, and we could not find that critical guiding light. I heard my mother whispering 'Help us, Lord Jesus, please help us!" She was praying in proper English, with a profound urgency to her tone. Suddenly a shadowy figure stepped out from behind a tree ahead of us; it was Uncle Egypt!

"Shush, now!" he whispered urgently, "*Come quick, now!*" He turned around, beckoning us to follow him. Holding hand, we ran behind him through the wet forest for about half a mile until we came to a clearing. There ahead of us was a covered wagon! It was filled with kegs of whiskey, baskets of corn, and Lord knows what else. But everything was packed so that the back of the wagon was empty; that is where we would be hiding.

The driver pulled out some of the baskets of corn, and we scrambled up into it, following his instruction to cover ourselves with some blankets that were waiting for us. He then re-packed the wagon, piling the baskets on top of us as we lay spooned into each other. To our surprise the baskets were light; that was because they were mostly packed with straw and layered with corn.

We never saw the face of the person driving the wagon, and he traveled at a moderate clip; no one stopped us because there was no one on the road—probably because of the rain and the holiday time. After several miles the wagon stopped and, assisted by the driver, we climbed out.

The driver gave us directions to the next stop and allowed us to take the blankets, gave us salted pork, biscuits, and a pretty hefty chunk of cheese. He also gave us directions to the next stop on the way. However, to get there, we had to walk quite a few miles through the wet and slippery woods; I figured it to be about 50 miles since that was what the quilt said. The wagon driver told us what markers and landmarks to look for, and wished us God-speed.

Shivering and wet, we headed into the woods, praying that we were going in the right direction and that we would not miss a marker. The rain drizzled off and on, compounding our distress as our clothes were pretty soaked by then. We were wearing our new set of clothing under the old ones; but, sloshing through the wet sometimes swampy undergrowth, we were soon reduced to dirty and raggedy bundles of rags. In addition to the food that the wagon driver gave us, each of us had a sack with food and what little else we could carry.

My father had stolen a knife and what else I don't know, but he also carried the pot for cooking, and the wooden bowls and spoons. My mother had made little sacks from pieces of yarn, which she filled with her precious dried herbs; in this way, she was able to keep them separated, and she could identify them all by scent and taste. She carried the sacks in her folded apron, the ends of which she tied around her waist so that it formed a pouch.

We trudged through the woods until the wee hours of the morning, feeling our way through the forest, and praying; we had no idea how far we had traveled and were very relieved whenever we found or stumbled upon a marker that confirmed that we were heading northward. When we finally came to the end of the woods, it was a little before dawn, and still very dark. We looked to the right, as the wagon driver instructed, and saw smoke curling from a chimney and a light in the window like he said; but there was a considerable distance between us and the farmhouse—and no trees between the woods and the dwelling that we could hide behind.

We crouched in the shadows trying to decide what to do. We chose to cling to the edge of the woods and follow it to see if it came any closer to the house than where we were. It was with great relief that we realized that the woods curved towards a barn behind the house. By that time, the dawn was breaking; a cock crowed and was answered by first one, then another. A dog barked, and a man carrying two wooden buckets entered the barn.

We were still uncertain about what to do so we stayed in the woods, watching and waiting for a sign that this was a safe-house. Eventually, two Negro women came out from a shed behind the house, each balancing a basketful of laundry on her hip. One by one they hung small pieces of clothing on the line; the very last thing they hung up was a quilt—with a big *Log Cabin* design in the middle of it.

The Log Cabin

Log Cabin © 2018 Richard Haynes
NOTE: All full color quilt paintings may be viewed at:
http://artistrichardhaynes.com/undergroundrailroad.html

The Log Cabin Quilt

This was the safe-house the wagon driver told us about. But we decided to wait until dark before we approached the house. We remained hidden in the woods and ate some of the biscuits and cheese. The rain had stopped, but the forests were still wet from the previous night's downpour, and we were pretty miserable all the while. However, we observed that toward the end of the day, even when one of the women fetched the rest of the laundry when the sun was low in the sky, the log cabin quilt remained on the line.

We were sure this was a safe-house. Finally, when night fell, we crept up to the house and knocked on the back door. To our surprise, it opened promptly, and a kindly older white woman stood there, smiling at us.

"Come on in, come on it!" she said, warmly. "My goodness, you must be so tired and hungry!" It was quite evident that she had been expecting us.

We piled into the warm kitchen and I, for one, felt my knees buckle as the scent of freshly baked bread surrounded me. My brothers look just as raggedy and hungry as I, but my parents tried to look composed; however, I could see the relief on their faces. Miss Maggie had long brown hair sprinkled liberally with grey, which she wore parted in the middle, and tied up in a bun. She had dancing hazel eyes and wore glasses perched on the end of her nose.

Miss Maggie promptly hustled us into a room in which a huge claw-footed bathtub full of hot water steamed. Four bundles of clean clothes were folded on a bench against the hallway wall outside of the bathing room. She instructed us to bathe ourselves quickly, change into the clean clothes, and then to return to the kitchen. She assured us that we were quite safe there, as no one came by at that time of the night and, indeed, hardly ever. Since it was the holidays, it would be days before anyone came looking for runaway slaves; we would be long gone by then, she assured us.

We had never bathed in a proper bathtub before, and with this new experience, we completely forgot to be hungry! We decided that Mother would be the first to wash, then my father. Homer went next, then me, and finally poor Isaac. By the time it was Isaac's turn, the water was still barely warm, but definitely brownish in color. Nevertheless, we were grateful and excited at having taken our very first proper bath; that, and the clean clothes uplifted us in spirit.

Back in the kitchen, there was a fire going in the big brick fireplace, and it had already consumed our filthy clothes. We sat down to a sumptuous meal of warm bread and soup made with root vegetables. Miss Maggie asked my father to say grace, and we all held hands as he thanked God for sending His angels to help us on our journey. He asked a sincere blessing upon Miss Maggie, and upon her household. It was the most delicious meal we had ever had…and we ate from a real bowl with real spoons.

As we ate, Miss Maggie told us that we were in Richmond, Virginia and that we were in the New Year of 1850. Within a few days we would be in Washington, home of President Zachary Taylor, she said. We realized that we had lost count of time and were quite shocked to learn that we had already passed through North Carolina.

She told us that she was a Quaker, of the Society of Friends, and that her home was a meeting house—as was the home of every Quaker because they did not believe in having specific buildings for worship. It was at the meetings that new strategies were planned to help fugitive slaves, and not a single runaway that passed through their Underground Railroad had every been recaptured; most went to Canada to safety, others settled in Baltimore, New York and such like states.

Secretly, she and her husband, the late Mr. Jeremiah Price, had been helping slaves escape to freedom for many years; however, he had gone to be with his Maker three years ago. Before he passed, he bought the two Negro women and freed them; the freed women took up the Quaker religion. They knew that many freed slaves were returned to slavery frequently through trickery, and they felt safe with the Quakers, so they chose to stay with Miss Maggie and were content to serve her as faithful friends.

The man that we had seen entering the barn was Miss Maggie's brother; we never saw him or the two women all the time we were there, although their efforts to help us were evident in the meals they prepared, and the fresh milk we drank every morning. We never saw them because—just in case they were ever questioned—Miss Maggie did not want them to have any information about any of the slaves; however, they knew of—and assisted in—some of the escape activities. For example, the women were responsible for hanging out the quilts every day, and her brother was responsible for notifying the next wagon driver of a pick-up when runaways found their way to the farm.

That night we slept in a large room in the cellar, in proper beds. The place was hidden behind a false wall, and there were six beds in that room; these were built by the late Mr. Price. That is where Miss Maggie hid us for two days, let us take baths in a real bathtub, sleep in proper beds, and eat all we wanted.

During that time, my mother continued to teach us reading and writing, and Miss Maggie supplied us with writing paper and elementary school books, which she kept in that room to help the runaways learn letters, numbers, or improve on skills they may have already possessed. While there, we took turns reading and thus improved on our rudimentary learning as we waited until another wagon came to pick us up for the next leg of the journey.

"It is almost a week since we escaped from the Thomsen plantation," my father said to Miss Maggie, "but it feels like years already! I think I know how Moses felt when he left Egypt and traveled 40 years before reaching the Promised Land." Miss Maggie laughed and said that we would be leaving Richmond— not Egypt—the following night and she sure hoped it wouldn't take us that long to reach freedom.

Since my mother was an accomplished reader, Miss Maggie gave her a book by a freed slave named Frederick Douglass[20], which he had published 3 years earlier. This was an account of his life as a slave, and it was to provide us with hope and cement our determination to reach Canaan Land for it reminded us of what we were leaving behind. We read and re-read that book several times on our journey and, because of that book, we did not become like the Hebrews after they left bondage in Egypt; we never longed for anything that we had left behind no matter how difficult the challenges we faced!

Mistress Haverhill had already explained to my mother what the Underground Railroad was and she had passed that knowledge on to us, so we understood when Miss Maggie told us her house was a station, and people like her and the wagon drivers were station masters and conductors—and our train was going straight to Canaan Land! Then she gave us instruction about what was to happen next.

We were to be picked up by another wagon and taken to a forested area. The wagon driver would give us directions to a creek, and we were to cross the stream and follow the signs that would lead to a cabin. If there was a Bear Paw's quilt on the rails of the small porch, we were at the right place. We were to wait

---

[20] Frederick Augustus Washington Bailey (1818?—1895): a former slave, abolitionist, and the first Black to hold a high-ranking position in the U.S. Government; author of several biographical books on his life as a slave.

there for the next conductor. That night, when the wagon picked us up, we traveled many miles, all night, before we were dropped off at the edge of a forest. Once again, our instructions were to follow identifying markers through the woods to the next stop.

The Bear's Paw

The Bear's Paw © 2018 Richard Haynes
NOTE: All full color quilt paintings may be viewed at:
http://artistrichardhaynes.com/undergroundrailroad.html

The Bear's Paw Quilt

The conductor arrived at nightfall just as Miss Maggie said he would. The wagon was filled with chickens in wooden cages and boxes of onions, and our hiding place was to the back of the cart, squeezed together like spoons. Once again we traveled many miles to the stop, huddled under foul-smelling blankets, barely able to breathe. The wagon rumbled along over rocky paths, jostling us so that it felt like our bones were rattling.

When we finally reached our destination just before dawn, the wagon driver gave us directions to the creek. We were to follow the markers until we got to a specific muddy spot, which was marked by a huge fallen moss-covered oak tree. From there we were to follow the animal tracks that led away from the mud, which would lead us to water. We were to look for an old cabin, which would be empty— but on the porch rails there would be a raggedy quilt with the Bear's Paw patch; that would confirm that we were where we were supposed to be. There would be food in the cabin and water was already available from the creek; we were to stay there until someone came for us.

It was on the way to the water that I started feeling sick. I was burning up but couldn't stop shivering. Father had to carry me on his back as I couldn't walk because of the fever. Mother looked so worried! She had brought along some of the medicinal herbs for fevers and colds that she kept in our cabin, but we would have no water for boiling until we came to the creek.

"Lord, the child is burning up!" Mother kept saying. She never sounded this afraid before; later, Mother told me that she was even more scared than when she knew she was going to get a beating from the Mistress or Master Thomsen's men. She kept saying something about her "penrile"[21] tea. This is the pennyroyal plant that the slaves dried and brewed into a tea to break the fevers in those days.

I remember my father saying "We'll get to water soon! When we get to the water, we will make some tea. I'm sure it will bring down his fever."

Father carried me immediately into the water when we got to the stream. There was no cabin in sight, so father told Mother and Homer to go right and follow the water until they found it, while he would stay with Isaac and tend to me. Mother didn't want to leave me, but father insisted that she and my brothers get a good drink of water and go look for that cabin. He didn't want to leave her alone by the stream with me in case of animals.

---

[21] Pennyroyal herb

Father got a fire going and started brewing the tea. He was wiping my face with a wet rag when two old white men came out of the woods to the clearing by the stream. They were just as shocked to see my father as he was to see them. Isaac clung to my father in fear.

The men were carrying rifles, but by their ragged clothing, my father could see that they were just poor whites hunting small game for food. Poor whites practically had it no better than us slaves; some of them felt sorry for the slaves, but most hated the slaves because they thought that they made it difficult for them to get work on the plantations or anywhere else. They had sacks slung across their shoulders in which they probably had whatever small game they could scrape up for food.

"Whut y'all doin' here, boy?" one of them snarled at my father. "Who you niggers belong to?" the other yelled.

My father put on his slave voice, speaking the way slaves usually did: "Dis here boy has de fever from de pox, suh, and dis' odder one is ketchin' it, too. Jest tryin' to cool down de fever, suh!" father told them, careful not to make eye contact.

"You get out of dat water right now, boy!" they ordered, pointing the rifles at my father. Father ignored them.

"Jest coolin' down de boy's fever, suh!" he repeated. "Dese here boys got de small pox, Suh!"

The two old men stopped dead in their tracks. If they had not caught the word *smallpox* before, they certainly heard it when my father said it that way the second time around. They backed up warily.

"Did you jest say *smallpox*, boy?"

"Yes, suh…*small pox*," my father responded, dragging out the word for emphasis, not looking at them. "Ole Marse sez for me to stay by dis here crick until dese here boys eidder get healed or die! An' he tole me not to say whut place I come from lessen it cause panic. But Ole Marse didn't give us no food, suh, jest dis little pot for ketching water…do you have *anyting* to spare, suh? Ah sure am hungry! And ah feels as if ah is ketchin' de smallpox too!"

The old men looked at each other and just turned and high-tailed it out of there like the devil was after them. They were not about to mess with anyone who carried the pox!

By this time Mother and Homer had returned but remain hidden in the bushes, watching all of this from their hiding place. As soon as the men were out of sight, Mother and Homer came toward them. When father told them about the exchange of words between him and the men, and how he spoke in "slave language", mother didn't know if to laugh or cry with relief; she hugged my father and said that God was extra merciful to us that day.

Mother and Homer led us to the cabin where mother made some more yarb tea; after drinking that tea a few times, my fever eventually broke sometime later. Father's eyes filled with tears because he had imagined having to bury and leave me behind in that place. I remember how he choked up when he said "I love you, son," as he held my hand tightly—while I squirmed as mother kissed me all over my face. Thomas and Isaac just stood there grinning at me and I suddenly realized how much I loved them all!

Just like with the other quilts, we knew that on the back of the patch would be a line of stitches heading off toward the right. Mother counted 75 stitches before there was a lump of thread. While we waited, we recollected our journey thus far; we talked about the animal tracks that led to the creek, and we wondered if whoever left the food and the quilt made those tracks for us because there were so many of them.

So, with our stomachs filled, with renewed hope and faith, with bowed heads we thanked the Good Lord for all His tender mercies shown to us and implored Him to cover us for the rest of our journey. We prayed blessings upon all who helped us, and all of those still waiting to receive us. We slept deeply—until we were awakened by the next conductor.

Shoo-Fly

Shoo-Fly © 2018 Richard Haynes
NOTE: All full color quilt paintings may be viewed at:
http://artistrichardhaynes.com/undergroundrailroad.html

The Shoo-Fly Quilt

Once again, for the next leg of the journey, we were hidden in a wagon covered against the raw weather. I don't know how far we traveled—but again we were being jostled about like bags of bones as we lay hidden under foul smelling blankets. This time the coverings reeked of onions as the wagon was loaded with crates of the vegetable…and some were rotted, too. That was because we had to travel through a populated area and the onion scent would deter bloodhounds if any were around.

The wagon driver said only one thing when we entered the wagon, and slapped his cheek: *Shoo-fly!* We thought that he had swatted a fly because there were a few around on account of the stench of the onions, but my mother said that that probably was a signal to look for the Shoo-fly quilt. We were headed to another station that was on the way to Washington where President Zachary Taylor lived.

We traveled for hours, and when the wagon finally stopped, we emerged into darkness. The driver instructed us to follow specific markers until we came to a cemetery on the border of town; we were to look for the kneeling angel statue atop a marble crypt and wait there. *Someone would come,* he said; it would be one of the slaves who kept the cemetery grounds.

The crypt with the kneeling angel statue was locked, so we crouched close to its cold marble walls, feeling scared and exposed. I don't remember how long it was that we waited there, cold, thirsty, hungry—and terrified that haints would rise up out of those graves and get us. We had left the cabin by the creek so quickly that we did not have time to eat or drink anything.

It was rainy and humid, and the mists that rose from the cemetery ground frightened us terribly. Then, suddenly, we saw a haint that seemed to be floating toward us! We were petrified and about to scatter in every direction when a voice said "*Shoo-fly!*" Before we knew it, the haint stood before us, wrapped in an old quilt, and there it was—the Shoo-fly patch! We had found the quilt! Or perhaps the quilt had found us...

Shoo-Fly turned out to be the nick-name of Willy Joe Barns, a free black man. He was 60 years old, thin, bald, and bony. He was the primary keeper for the cemetery and knew the rhythm of that sacred place. He knew when there were to be funerals, and when grieving family members visited the graves of their loved ones. He held the keys to all of the crypts and hid our family in the weeping angel crypt, as family members visited it only once a year; it was a sacred and safe place. Best of all, Shoo-fly had left food and water there for us!

We hid in that place for a day, eating the food Shoo-Fly gave us and napped a bit. My mother read to us from Frederick Douglass's book, and we waited and prayed. When Willy came with more supplies that night, my father looked at him with tears in his eyes and said "Mr. Willy, Sir, thank you for your kindness and your bravery. God bless you, Mr. Willy, for risking your life to help us and others." Shoo-fly grasped my father's hands firmly, nodded with a sad smile, and left.

That night, when he came with more supplies, Shoo-fly told us that following night he would come to lead us to where another wagon would be waiting to take us to Washington. He would take us to a building that was a merchandise business owned by an abolitionist. We were to go to the shop that had the Bow-Tie quilt hanging in the window.

The Bow-Tie

Bow-Tie © 2018 Richard Haynes
NOTE: All full color quilt paintings may be viewed at:
http://artistrichardhaynes.com/undergroundrailroad.html

The Bow Tie Quilt

We transferred to three or four different wagons on the way to Washington and, days later it seemed, we arrived at the merchandise shop with the Bow-Tie quilt displayed in the window; it was the Washington business of David Hall, a prominent businessman, and abolitionist.

Once safely inside, he led us to the cellar where there was water and clean clothes—we sorely needed to wash up, and change our stinky clothing. He told us the message of the Bow-Tie quilt was that we needed to clean up to blend into a city. That secret room in his cellar was big enough to hold at least 10 people, but at that time we were the only occupants. He gave us new clean clothes from his shop, and we felt very rich and grand, indeed!

We had to stay there for a few days as by then the rains turned to snow, and it was too unsafe to continue the journey. During that time, Mother continued to read the Frederick Douglas book and teach us reading, writing, and counting. Mr. Hill supplied us with a newspaper, quill pens and ink, and writing paper. It was during that time in Mr. Hall's cellar that mother told us all she knew of her history, and why Mistress Thomsen was so cruel to her. She explained to us that before me and my brothers were born, there was another baby, a girl, and the circumstances of her birth. That child belonged to Master Thomsen.

When she was about 13 years old, Master Thomsen came down to the kitchen where mother was sleeping and woke her up. He took her to a hut down by where the stables were, and hurt her. He had a lock for that hut, and nobody but he used it. She screamed throughout the ordeal. She knew others heard her, but no one dared to help. She told us it wasn't the first time that she had to endure what Master did to her in that locked room.

Then, when she started throwing up every morning, Cook told her that she had a baby growing in her and that, for sure, the Mistress would not like that. Sure enough, when the child was born, Mistress saw the color of the child and how it was not like the other black babies; she figured out right away that her husband fathered the child because Chrissy always worked close to the house and was constantly under Cook's watchful eye, and nobody else could have had that opportunity.

Mistress made her husband take that child away that same day she was born—and my mother never saw her baby girl again. My mother had named that child *Charlotte* after her mother and never knew what became of her. It was as if my mother lost her mother all over again when she lost Baby Charlotte. It was then that Mistress Thomsen started abusing my mother—it broke my mother's heart, but not her spirit; from that time my mother started dreaming of running away, but she didn't know how. That desire only grew as the abuses continued.

Mother told us that it was after her baby was taken away that she started learning about yarb doctoring because she wanted to know which herbs would kill a person. In her 13 or 14-year old mind, she thought it would be just punishment for whatever Mistress Thomsen did to her baby, and for the daily abuses that the woman heaped on her. But God intervened and prevented her from making a terrible mistake by having my father marry her.

The abuse only stopped after mother jumped the broom with my father, which was just about the time that Mistress Haverhill took up residence at the Thomsen plantation. Mistress Haverhill took my mother as her personal maid after my mother made her some yarb tea to heal a cough that wouldn't go away— and that was fine with Mrs. Thomsen because Mother would be out of her sight most of the time.

When the time was drawing close for us to continue on our journey, Mr. Hall informed us that the next stop would be at a quilt-maker's little shop in one of the busiest parts of the city; it was called *A Stitch in Time Quilt Shoppe*. This was the final stop in the Pennsylvania leg of the journey, but this stop could be different from the others as we would have to look carefully to see which quilt pattern was in the window. If it was the *North Star*, then the path was clear to travel north to Canada. However, if the zigzagging *Drunkard's Path* quilt was hanging in the window that would that signified trouble because that pattern meant that it was not safe to be in the area: slave catchers were around!

Drunkard's Path

Drunkard's Path © 2018 Richard Haynes
NOTE: All full color quilt paintings may be viewed at:
http://artistrichardhaynes.com/undergroundrailroad.html

The Drunkard's Path Quilt

Mr. Hall explained that because of the presence of many free slaves in Pennsylvania, and because runaways always tried to blend into the populace in such places, every Negro in that State was suspected of being a fugitive and could be stopped and questioned by slave catchers at any time. Sometimes, legally freed slaves were recaptured and taken back into captivity, so we were all acutely aware that this was a dangerous part of our journey.

If the Drunkard's path quilt were hanging in the window, we would have to change our itinerary so that we would travel southward for a while, then reverse direction back to northward, and continue doing this for a bit, until it was safe to head northward once again. That thought terrified us. My mother had to grasp the back of a chair to steady herself—just the idea of going in a southward direction frightened her so much that she felt faint.

Then Mr. Hall informed us that we would be traveling by day and that we were to head out *"bright and early in the morning."* It would be the second time that we would be journeying in the daytime, and we were petrified by the thought! That night we hardly slept, fretting about the upcoming journey. We arose to a gloomy day with a light snowfall as we headed toward the Stitch in Time Quilt Shoppe in one of Mr. Hall's carriages.

Mr. Hall was a prominent man in town, and no one would have suspected that he was a station master in the Underground Railroad. Because of his respectable position in that community, none of his carriages had ever been stopped for inspection. Besides, several Negroes worked in the Hall residence, and he gave the deliberate impression that he owned them when, in truth, they were all free—having been runaways themselves! We marveled at Mr. Hall's coolness and his bravery in conducting that section of the Underground Railroad system.

As we got closer to the quilt shop, which was sandwiched between a barber shop and a confectionary, we all held our breath. The carriage rumbled by without slowing down. As we passed by, we could see that the pattern on the quilt in the window was that of the swirly Drunkard's Path. Our hearts sank; that was one of the most frightening moments for me because from that instance I felt as if every white face we passed belonged to a slave catcher out to get me!

Now began the confusing zigzag as we headed South, then North again, repeating the pattern several times. The final stop on that leg of the journey was at a Pennsylvania border town where the North Star quilt was hanging from a rack as part of a tableau in the window of a furniture maker's establishment. We knew that from there on the journey would only be northward. For days we traveled nonstop through Maryland, Delaware, and Pennsylvania, changing modes of transportation and conductors along the way. We were guided by the North Star pattern on quilts that hung from the fences, clotheslines, and porches of farmhouses, or the windows of seamstresses or merchandise stores.

In Pennsylvania, Mr. Hall had told us that when we saw the *Crossroads* quilt hanging from the window at another seamstress's establishment, we would know that we were at a point where we would have to make an important decision. We would have to consult with our conductor on whether to choose the route to Canada through New York or Ohio, or whether to go through the Northeastern states through New Jersey, Connecticut, New Hampshire, into Vermont—then to Canaan Land.

Crossroads

Crossroads © 2018 Richard Haynes
NOTE: All full color quilt paintings may be viewed at:
http://artistrichardhaynes.com/undergroundrailroad.html

The Crossroads Quilt

When we finally arrived at the crossroad of our journey at the seamstress establishment, our conductor decided that we would take the path through Vermont as the one through New York and Ohio were the ones most traveled, and there was a heavy presence of slave catchers along those routes.

Along the way, we crossed rivers and lakes on boats and, when frozen, on sleds. We rode in carriages and wagons, and posed as servants and sometimes had to split up, which caused my parents great anxiety. Once, we boys had to dress up as girls when my mother read a notice of runaway slaves whose descriptions we fit. We boys did not like that at all!

As we traveled, during the day, in some places, we saw free slaves and wondered what their daily lives were like. These people seemed to walk more proudly, and they did not shuffle and bow and scrape like those we had left behind. We saw children playing and heard their laughter ring through the air. *Was this freedom?* I wondered.

The New England air was crisp and clean; at night, the skies above the snow-clad Northern states were something to behold!

They seemed to be brighter, and the stars seemed to sparkle more brilliantly. Us boys learned to identify the Big and Little Dippers, the Plough, the Three Sisters and other constellations. I used to marvel that that same sky that covered us also covered our brethren, still in slavery, in the South. And, as we traveled, every night we sought out the North Star, which assured us that, indeed, we were journeying toward Canada, our Canaan Land.

Chapter 5

North through New England

We crossed creeks spanned by covered bridges and were mesmerized by the gently rolling snow-covered hills of New England. It was magical to see how the snows sparkled like diamonds under a full moon, and how graceful and pretty the evergreen trees looked wearing their mantles of soft white snow. All along our journey through the Southern states, we stayed in farmhouses, cabins, and once even in a crypt! As we journeyed through the Northern states, our stations were businesses, Churches, farmhouses, Meeting Houses, and elegant homes of gentlemen and society women.

In Farmington, Connecticut, we stayed for a day and a night at the home of the devoted abolitionist, Mr. Austin F. Williams, sleeping in a room prepared for freed and escaped slaves, in their carriage house. In Bedford, Massachusetts, we spent two days at the home of Mr. and Mrs. Nathan Johnson, who were Quakers.

We were delighted to learn that our hero, Mr. Frederick Douglass had also stayed there a few years earlier in 1838. We were told that there were more than 300 free slaves and their families living in New Bedford and that the men were engaged in whaling and the maritime trades. My father seriously considered settling us there, but my mother prevailed on him to continue the journey to Canada, as the reach of slave catchers extended even to this place.

We arrived in Portsmouth, New Hampshire, and were immediately taken to Lee, New Hampshire, to the home of Mr. Moses Cartland. One of my fondest memories was of our stay at the Cartland residence [22]. He was a Quaker and a strident voice for the abolition of slavery. Once again, tempted by the kindness and generosity of this Quaker, we were almost persuaded to stay and work for him—for real wages.

We ended up staying there until the spring, doing household and other chores, as well as continuing our learning. During that time, Father and us boys built a beautiful armoire for Mrs. Cartland, and Mother and Mrs. Cartland sewed a quilt with all of the patches that held the codes of the Underground Railroad. Mother taught Mrs. Cartland many of our plantation spirituals, and it was a blessed thing to hear their voices blend in song!

---

[22] The Cartland House is one of six prominent stations on the Underground Railroad: http://www.newenglandhistoricalsociety.com/6-stops-underground-railroad/

By this time my father and us boys were able to read from the Frederick Douglass book, even though our mother had to help us through some big words. It was also during that time that Isaac stopped having nightmares in his sleep; these had begun the night of the Lewis murder. He did not scream or make noise but held his terror within so that his body would jerk as he slept, and the tears wet his pillow. It felt so good to settle into a routine that seemed like that of a real home; however, once again, my mother prevailed and, eventually, we had to press on. I came to realize that there was no place in America that my mother could ever feel safe.

I fell in love with the New England countryside then, and came to love New Hampshire mainly because of the warmth and generosity of Mr. Cartland in Lee, for we stayed at his residence the longest, and came to know him best among all the folks who helped us along the way. He had read Frederick Douglass's book and held open discussions with people of like mind at his home, and encouraged us to tell our stories. Many wept openly when my parents recounted the murder of poor Lewis and resolved to redouble their efforts to help their enslaved brothers and sisters; however, of all the stories we told, Mother never mentioned that of our lost baby sister, Charlotte.

When in the spring of 1950 we finally arrived in Vermont, my mother finally relaxed visibly. The lines in her face softened, and she smiled a lot. When I thought about it, I had not seen her smile, or hear her laugh, since the day we witnessed poor Lewis' murder. I realized for the first time that my mother was a beautiful woman, and watching how her laughter brought joy to my father's face made me realize how much he loved this brave woman.

In Vermont, I was awestruck by those mighty rolling hills, and somehow that made it seem closer to heaven. This was the first State to abolish slavery in 1777; however, slave catchers ventured even there and could capture and re-enslave runaways— and even some freed slaves, as they did in the other Northern States. I never could have imagined that such a place as Lee and Vermont existed. Crossing the mountains sometimes terrified me, and sometimes made me want to shout and sing.

We stayed at the Rokeby[23] place in Ferrisburgh, Vermont. Mr. Rowland T. Robinson owned the estate, which his parents built. He was a passionate abolitionist who openly harbored runaways and freed slaves. He helped them find jobs and negotiated freedom for many of these fugitives.

---

[23] One of the verified stations on the Underground Railroad

Once again, though so close to Canada, my father was tempted to set roots in this place. But one night, my mother took my father to a hill behind the farmhouse and pointed north: "Over there," she said, "is the Promised Land. I am willing to die here right now for you to get to that Promise Land with our sons." And that is how we ended up crossing Lake Champlain to the Canadian side—to Canaan Land!

(The Canadian Flag 1801 – 1965)

Chapter 6

Life in British Canada: 1850 –

Yes, we followed that North Star all the way to Canada and freedom. I was 14 years old when we entered Canaan Land in the summer of 1850. With the help of the Presbyterian Church and the Quakers, we traveled from Montreal to Buxton and right into the Elgin Settlement[24].

The Reverend William King had established Buxton just one year before our entry into Canada in 1849 as a refuge for former slaves. Reverend King was an abolitionist who married a Southern belle. She bore him a child, but soon she and the child died. Then his father-in-law also passed away, and he inherited land and 15 slaves from his estate.

When the Presbyterian Church assigned him to Canada, Reverend King decided to take his slaves with him, rather than leave them for, even if he freed them, they could be re-enslaved as that occurred quite often. He purchased land near Chatham,

---

[24] http://www.blackhistorycanada.ca

Ontario for $2.50 per acre and established Buxton, also known as the Elgin Settlement, as a refuge for slaves seeking freedom in Canada.

It was as if God led us straight to that Settlement because Reverend King's dream was to provide the former slaves with a good education to prepare them for the opportunities that freedom brought. My mother had already taught us the rudimentary skills in reading, writing, and numbers, which we practiced along the journey to freedom, so we were able to fit right in as students.

The quality of education at the Settlement rose to such a high standard that eventually, the schools for white children were closed and the children were sent to school at Elgin, making these learning institutions the first integrated schools in North America.

Mother and Father were determined that their children would learn as much as possible, so she continued to teach us. Reverend King immediately recognized her talent in these areas and appointed her to be a teacher while providing her with additional lessons that improved her skills. My mother was tireless in her efforts to help educate former slaves and even taught night classes several times a week in addition to teaching during the day.

Mother also taught spinning, weaving, and quilting. At each session, she repeated the story of the quilts and how they whispered their messages of direction and hope as they pointed us to freedom, and how they warned us of impending or present danger. She taught anyone who wanted to learn how to stitch those quilts patterns, and many were eager to learn as their experiences with the whispering quilts were similar to our own. She instructed them to tell their children and grandchildren their stories and the message of the quilt—and at the bottom of each final quilt patch, she embroidered the words "Ahosi Mino" in honor of her mother.

We could have taken up new names once we got to freedom in Canada, but we did not. My father and Homer wanted to do it, but our mother would have none of it. She said that she hated that name, but that name also bound us to others who could have been her brothers and sisters, or our father's brothers and sisters. They would have been born on that plantation, but perhaps sold to another.

You see, although my mother never knew who they were, she always believed that she had siblings on the Thomsen Plantation as well as on other plantations because she knew that her father was a stock slave and, just like she did, she believed that others carried his blood in their veins also. And for that reason, mother insisted we keep the Thomsen name in case others from that plantation escaped to freedom in Canada and found their way to the Elgin Settlement.

My mother always asked newly arrived slaves if they ever lived on the Thomsen Plantation. She reminded us that slaves carried the names of their owners, so we kept the Thomsen name because that's how it was then; besides, we didn't know any other name. In a way, this name binds us to Master Thomsen as long as we exist on this earth. However, it was like one of those quilt-patterns pointing us to our ancestor and to lost family members, and guiding them to us. If they made it to Canada where we were, they would know that they had friends or family in this new land, she said.

Chapter 7

Passages

My mother lived to be a ripe old age and saw the birth of many grandchildren. She passed in 1899, and my daddy followed soon after in 1900. Homer stayed in Canada and grew the carpenter business that he and my father started together and that creative blood runs through all of his children; they became artists, builders, and teachers.

I was newly married with a newborn baby when the Civil War that ended slavery started in America; that was in 1861. There was not a man or woman there at the Settlement who did not pray daily for the cause of President Lincoln to be established by the Good Lord, and when the North won, children, you never seen so much jumping and shouting and rejoicing as that day when we heard that blessed news! Ah, but what weeping followed the announcement of President Lincoln's assassination! I guess his work was all done and the Lord just wanted him back up there with Him where he belonged!

During Reconstruction, my brother Isaac returned to America as he had heard about opportunities available to blacks; but in the end that didn't turn out so well because the Ku Klux Klan in their white hoods terrorized the poor blacks so! Lord, what terrible news reached us here in Canada about the goings-on over there, and we feared for poor Isaac's life every day.

We begged Isaac to come back to Canada, but although he visited us whenever he could, Isaac felt a great obligation to return to that land of our enslavement to help our people, and education was the only way out, he said. So, he became a teacher and married the daughter of an escaped slave. She grew up in New York and got educated there; together, they founded a school that produced some fine minds, from what I heard. Isaac is buried there, but he and his children sure left their mark on Charleston, and there is even a building named after one of them, from what I hear!

So, my children, this is my story, and it is your story, too. I know that, as a people, our struggle continues to this day; but as long as you are willing to look up, hold fast to the good Lord, move forward, and never lose hope, you will reach your destination—you will achieve your goals.

Chapter 8

James Thomsen, II: Narrative Update (2017)

I am the great-grandson of Thomas Thomsen who was born a slave in 1836. At 88 years old in 1924, as a free man, this ancestor of mine penned the story of his escape with his parents and two brothers from a Southern plantation in 1849 to freedom in Canada in 1850. For many years I sought to uncover aspects of my ancestors' lives that eluded Great-grandpa Thomas and his parents—and even his children. Because we carry the DNA of our ancestors in our bodies, and because technologies exist that unlock its secrets, today I know what my mother and my ancestors did not.

My research led me to the roots of my grandmother, Charlotte, four times removed. Her homeland was the Kingdom of Dahomey in West Africa, which is today, Benin. I gained a deeper understanding of Charlotte's life on the slave ship that brought her to America; it took two to three months, depending on the weather, to complete the Middle Passage journey. These are some of the things I learned:

Like the other African nations and slave suppliers, the Kingdom of Dahomey fought wars with other African kingdoms and tribes, enslaving the peoples that they conquered. The Dahomeans traded those captives they did not need with the Europeans in exchange for guns, knives, guns, ammunition, textiles, tools, and other goods. They also conducted raids with the specific purpose of capturing and selling Africans to the Europeans[25].

From the start of the American slave trade in 1619 when the first slaver brought about 20 Africans to Point Comfort, Virginia, which was, at the time, a British colony, to the time of her capture in the latter 1700s, the lucrative slave trade had already been a fully established commercial enterprise that was more than 180-years-old. This traffic in the sons and daughters of Africa contributed to the Kingdom of Dahomey's wealth and prosperity.

Since Dahomey was a dominant kingdom in that part of Africa, and since she was the wife of a king, I don't know how Charlotte came to be among the captives who were traded in 1800; however, she was among those 200 or more slaves conquered or stolen from various parts of Africa and transported to the New

---

[25] Adandozan was King of Dahomey (1797-1818) at the time of the capture of the slave girl in the late 18th Century.

World. I learned from my visit to that area several years ago that the two words that Charlotte repeated throughout her life on the Thomsen Plantation were not her name; they were powerful declarations of who she *was*.

Charlotte was *Ahosi*, a wife of the King of Dahomey; she was also *Mino*, one of the King's warriors, later described by Europeans as African Amazons, who were selected only from among the Ahosi. As the wife of the King, she was royalty, and as a royal warrior, she would have carried an undying loyalty to her King to her grave; she would have been conditioned and committed to maintaining that fidelity to her King under every circumstance. *That* is why she could never submit to forced pregnancies, or accept the babies she birthed; she was the warrior wife of a king, and could never succumb to being a slave!

It is sobering to reflect on what it was like for Charlotte and the many captives on that slave ship. Customarily, they were put in shackles and brought to the ports along the coast, which came to be known as the *Slave Coast*. There, they were put on the big ships that would take them across the vast Atlantic Ocean to work the fields and plantations of the Americas.

It had to have been a terrifying experience for these poor souls. The slavers prodded them like cattle onto the vessel and piled them below deck, in the dark, musky hull of the ship. They crammed as many Africans as possible into this miserable space because they knew some would die on the long journey across the oceans.

In fact, because as many as one-third of the captives died on these voyages, many slavers packed their human cargo like sardines in a can, hoping to get a good profit from the survivors. This method was called "tight packing". Other slavers employed "loose packing" in which fewer Africans were transported to avoid overcrowding and the diseases spawned by the overpacking method; they hoped that less crowding would increase the survival rates of the human cargo, and, of course, their profits.

Since most of the Africans were captured deep inland where the different tribes lived in villages and had never even seen the sea, they were terrified and got sea-sick. The stench of their vomit, urine, and disease surrounded them in that dark hull and permeated the entire ship. Day after day, all day long, those poor souls had to crouch or lie down side by side, chained in leg-irons and soaked in their filth and vomit because they could not get to the buckets that were supposed to be their toilets.

The male slaves were kept chained in pairs because the traders were afraid that these men would mutiny and kill them all. Also, they didn't want them jumping off the ship and drowning because that was like watching money disappear right before their eyes.

The men were kept separate from the women and children and, if the weather permitted, they were brought up on deck so that the hulls could be cleaned; at this time, the slaves were washed and made to exercise. The traders threw buckets of water on the slaves to wash the filth off their bodies. This was an attempt to reduce sickness because down in that stinking hull, diseases such as dysentery (which they called the *flux*), fever, smallpox, scurvy, and various diseases were common among the shackled slaves.

For exercise—and, I suspect, perhaps for entertainment—once on deck, the traders terrorized the captives with their long whips, forcing them to run around, jump up and down, or "dance." Sometimes, though chained in pairs, some slaves were able to throw themselves overboard because they would rather be dead than endure that terrible, frightening journey. Their main meal was *dabbadabb*; this was a concoction of ground corn, to which salt, malagetta spice, and palm oil were added and boiled to the consistency of pudding[26]. They were fed twice a day, and every so often some slaves refused to eat; at these times, the traders force-fed them. *Ah, the suffering of our people!*

Charlotte's journey from Africa to South Carolina took her through the Middle Passage; this was the voyage from the African Slave Coast to the West Indies and to South and North America. Although many people died on that awful crossing, she survived. And because she survived, I survived, and so long as any of her descendants survive, the warrior spirit of that *Ahosi*, that *Mino*, will persist through them, triumphant over the evil that sought to dehumanize her and break her spirit.

My great-great-grandmother Chrissy would have been proud to know that her grandchildren and their children never lost that hunger for learning. They followed their North Star, and today her progeny are artists, builders, and educators. Some of us went back to South Carolina and left our stamp on the unique architecture of the place.

Chrissy healed with herbs in the 19th century, but in the 20th century, my mother's (Chrissy's great-grandchild) way of healing

---

[26] Based on descriptions in Captain Thomas Phillips' journal of the voyage of the HANNIBAL, 1693, in addition to *dabbadabb*, boiled horse-beans were also served on slave ships.

was through guiding and encouraging disadvantaged black and white men, women, and children to escape the shackles and bondage of their economic conditions through education. She was a social worker whose desire was to help keep African American families together. Just like in slavery days, these families are often torn apart by a new slave master, which is, too frequently, an unjust legal and economic system that arbitrarily destroys the family by unfair incarceration[27], and denial of equal opportunities.

And, following in that teaching and healing tradition, today I, James Thomsen II, descendant of former slaves, am an artist who uses my talent to tell the human stories of struggle, hope, and survival[28]. I created this quilt series to honor those slave ancestors who dared to risk their lives in pursuit of freedom from slavery. With these paintings, I also acknowledge the abolitionists without whom it would not have been possible for most of the runaway

---

[27] Of the approximately 10.7 million Africans brought to the New World, approximately 388,000 were shipped directly to North America (H.L. Gates, 2013). In 2014, African Americans constituted 2.3 million (34%) of the total 6.8 million correctional population. African Americans are 6 times more likely than Whites to be incarcerated for the same crime. (https://www.naacp.org/criminal-justice-fact-sheet/)

[28] The character of the artist, James II, is based on New Hampshire artist Richard Haynes, who depicted the quilt patches referenced in the story in his own unique art form.

slaves to follow the North Star to their Canaan Land. Through my paintings, in a sense, the quilts are whispering still.

A Personal Note

---·---

Thank you, dear Reader, for choosing my very first historical fiction novel, Whispering Quilts, as one of your reading choices! If you enjoyed it (and I sure hope you did!) please consider leaving a review on Amazon.

Every author values feedback from their readers as it encourages us and helps us understand our craft from your perspective. My goal is to write historical novels that represent truthfully conditions at the time, and also to remind us of the kindness and greatness that lies in the hearts and minds of our fellowmen – especially during the most trying times. If I have accomplished this goal, your review will be my reward.

May you continue to read purposefully and may your days be filled with joy as you follow your North Star

R. M. Tappin

RESOURCES

A slave is tortured. (1998). *New Hampshire PBS*. Retrieved from
https://www.pbs.org/wgbh/aia/part3/3h1516t.html

African American Heritage and Ethnography. (n.d). Africans in the low
country: Time, space, & people. *National Park Service, U.S. Dept.
of the Interior*. Retrieved from
https://www.nps.gov/ethnography/aah/aaheritage/index.htm

Burns, E. & Bouchard, S. (2003). *Underground Railroad sampler*. USA:
Quilt in a Day, Inc.

Drew, B. (2004). *Refugees from slavery: Autobiographies of fugitive slaves in
Canada*. New York: Dover Publications, Inc.

Franklin, J.H, & Schweninger, L. (1999). *Runaway slaves: Rebels on the
plantation*. New York: Oxford University Press.

Gates, H.L. (2013). The African Americans: How many slaves landed in
the U.S.? Retrieved from http://www.pbs.org/wnet/african-
americans-many-rivers-to-cross/history/how-many-slaves-
landed-in-the-us/

History on the net. (2018). Living conditions of slaves in the south:
Black peoples of America. Retrieved from
https://www.historyonthenet.com/living-conditions-of-
slaves/

Hurmence, B. (1984). *My folks don't want me to talk about slavery*. (1984).
ed. Homer F. Blair Publisher.

International Slavery Museum. (2018). History of the slave trade: Life
abroad the slave ships. Retrieved from
http://www.liverpoolmuseums.org.uk/ism/slavery/middle_pa
ssage/

Library of Congress. (2003). A century of lawmaking for a new nation:
U.S. congressional documents and debates. Retrieved from

http://www.loc.gov/rr/program/bib/ourdocs/13thamendme
nt.html

National Archives. (2018). America's historical documents: 13th
Amendment to the U.S. constitution: Abolition of slavery
(1865). Retrieved from https://www.archives.gov/historical-
docs/13th-amendment

Network to freedom: Evolution of the term "underground' railroad".
(2011). *National Park Service.* Retrieved from
https://www.nps.gov/subjects/ugrr/discover_history/evoluti
on-of-the-term.htm

South Carolina Estates. (2018). Drayton Hall Plantation – West Ashley
– Charleston County. Retrieved from https://south-carolina-
plantations.com/charleston/drayton-hall.html

Thomas, V. M. (1997). *Lest we forget: The passage from Africa to slavery to
emancipation.* New York, N.Y.: Crown Publishers, Inc.

Tobin, J. & Dobard, R.G. (2000). *Hidden in plain view: A secret story of
quilts and the Underground Railroad.* New York, NY: Anchor
Books.

Trinkley, M. (2018). South Carolina – African-Americans – Houses
that offered little cover. *SCIWAY: South Carolina's Information
Highway.* Retrieved from
https://www.sciway.net/afam/slavery/houses.html

About the Author

Dr. R.M. Tappin holds a Ph.D. in Business Management and Organization, with a specialization in Management Education.

Her first historical fiction novella, Whispering Quilts, is about a slave family attempting to flee the brutality of a South Carolina Plantation in the mid-1800s. They are helped by abolitionists and guided by coded quilt patterns, which signal warnings of danger or safety; failing to interpret the patterns correctly can result in recapture, brutal punishments, or death. Will they make it?

Other works in progress by Dr. Tappin are listed in the Upcoming Works Section of this book.

Contact: tappinbooks@aol.com
Facebook: www.facebook.com/rmtappinauthor
Twitter: https://twitter.com/rmtappin_author
Website: www.rmtappin.net
Note: Upcoming blog will be at: rmtappinauthor.com

About the Illustrator

Artist Richard Haynes

Richard Haynes is the Associate Director of Admissions for Diversity at the University of New Hampshire and is an accomplished and acclaimed artist. He is an American visual storyteller, a cultural keeper and maker. Richard uses his art not only to make society aware of the invisible in this world but also to provoke unity; his art reflects his colorful and diverse life. He is also a photographer, educator, lecturer, mentor, and a strong advocate for social justice.

Whispering Quilts was based on a series of quilt paintings rendered by Richard Haynes, which illustrate the story. These paintings convey the hidden messages on which fugitive slaves relied to be guided to freedom in the northern states and Canada. A signed and beautifully boxed limited edition set of the paintings and the story may be purchased by contacting the artist directly.

Contact: Richard.haynes@unh.edu
Website: www.artistrichardhaynes.com

117

IMAGES OF SLAVERY
From Africa to America

(All images are in the public domain and courtesy of the Library of Congress and the New York Public Library Free Digital Collection. The images are arranged in a "logical" order that reflects the events depicted in Whispering Quilts. These events take the reader through the slave journey as it might have been experienced by Charlotte and her progeny; from Africa to America, and to freedom in Canada)

Map of the Kingdom of Dahomey (Benin)

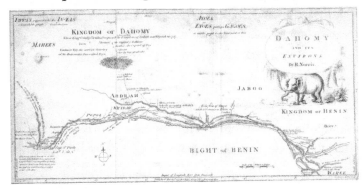

Schomburg Center for Research in Black Culture, Manuscripts, Archives and Rare Books Division, the New York Public Library. (1793). *Dahomy and its environs by R. Norris* Retrieved from http://digitalcollections.nypl.org/items/510d47dc-8779-a3d9-e040-e00a18064a99

Dahomean Women Warriors

(With Heads of Conquered Foes along a Wall)

(*Note:* In the public domain)

March to the Salve Coast: Africans Bound for Slavery in the New World

SLAVE TRADERS MARCHING THEIR CAPTIVES TO THE COAST. BUTCHERING DISABLED ONES ALONG THE WAY.

Schomburg Center for Research in Black Culture, Jean Blackwell Hutson Research and Reference Division, The New York Public Library. (1902 - 1902). *Slave traders marching their captives to the coast. Butchering disabled ones along the way.* Retrieved from http://digitalcollections.nypl.org/items/510d47de-0059-a3d9-e040-e00a18064a99

The Brooks Slave Ship (1789): Tight Packing of Human Cargo

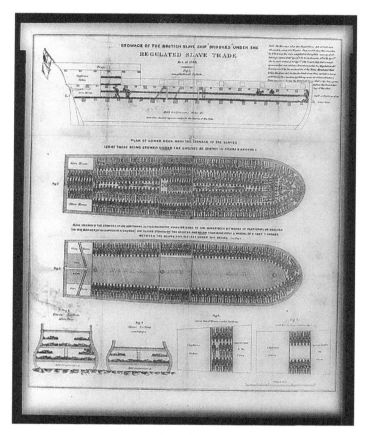

Note: in the public domain.

The Transatlantic Voyage: Slaves Forced to Dance

Schomburg Center for Research in Black Culture, Photographs and Prints Division, The New York Public Library. (1800). *Forcing captives to dance*. Retrieved from http://digitalcollections.nypl.org/items/510d47db-b9ae-a3d9-e040-e00a18064a99

[NOTE: Slaves were forced to dance for exercise and for the amusement of the Slavers]

Abroad a Slave Ship: Captured Africans Flogged to Make Them Eat and Sing

HE APPLIED THE LASH NOT ONLY TO MAKE THEM EAT BUT TO MAKE THEM SING.

Aboard a Slave Ship: Treatment of a 15-year-old Girl

Cruikshank, I. (1792) *The abolition of the slave trade Or the inhumanity of dealers in human flesh exemplified in Captn. Kimber's treatment of a young Negro girl of 15 for her virjen sic modesty.* , 1792. [London: Pubd. by S.W Fores] [Photograph] Retrieved from the Library of Congress, https://www.loc.gov/item/98510128/

Map of the British American Colonies Circa 1800

A map of the dominions of the King of Great Britain on ye continent of North America, containing Newfoundland, New Scotland, New England, New York, New Jersey, Pensilvania, Maryland, Virginia and Carolina.

[In the public domain. Retrieved from the Library of Congress, https://www.loc.gov/item/gm71005441/]

Settlers Landing at James Towne, 1607

The Miriam and Ira D. Wallach Division of Art, Prints and
Photographs: Picture Collection, the New York Public Library.
(1839). *Landing at Jamestown* Retrieved from
http://digitalcollections.nypl.org/items/510d47e0-f33b-a3d9-e040-
e00a18064a99

1619: Landing Africans at Jamestown

LANDING NEGROES AT JAMESTOWN
FROM DUTCH MAN-OF-WAR, 1619

(1901) *Landing Negroes at Jamestown from Dutch man-of-war.*, 1901.
[Photograph] Retrieved from the Library of Congress,
https://www.loc.gov/item/2005696251/.

Announcement of Sale of Slaves Circa 1700s

TO BE SOLD on board the Ship *Bance-Island*, on tuesday the 6th of *May* next, at *Ashley-Ferry*; a choice cargo of about 250 fine healthy NEGROES, just arrived from the Windward & Rice Coast. —The utmost care has already been taken, and shall be continued, to keep them free from the least danger of being infected with the SMALL-POX, no boat having been on board, and all other communication with people from *Charles-Town* prevented.

Austin, Laurens, & Appleby.

N. B. Full one Half of the above Negroes have had the SMALL-POX in their own Country.

Announcement of the arrival and sale of slaves from the Windward and Rice Coast. Such slaves were suited to the area due to the similarities in the geography of the plantations to the African rice-growing areas.
Retrieved from http://loc.gov/pictures/resource/cph.3a52072/

129

Public Notice of Slaves for Sale, 1784

NEGROES FOR SALE

A CARGO OF very ſtout Men and Women, in good order and fit for immediate ſervice, just imported from the Windward Coaſt of Africa, in the Ship TWO BROTHERS.

Conditions are one half Caſh or Produce, the other half payable the firſt of January next, giving Bond and Security if required.

May 19, 1784

John Mitchell

Schomburg Center for Research in Black Culture, Photographs and Prints Division, The New York Public Library. *Negroes for Sale.*" Retrieved from http://digitalcollections.nypl.org/items/83d2bf90-171e-4691-e040-e00a18061227

Branding Irons: Charleston, NC

Schomburg Center for Research in Black Culture,
Photographs and Prints Division, The New York Public
Library. *Branding irons, Charleston, N.C.* Retrieved from
http://digitalcollections.nypl.org/items/83d502af-b5bc-63e4-
e040-e00a1806171b

Branding of Female Slave

BRANDING A NEGRESS AT THE RIO PONGO
From a wood engraving in Canot's *Twenty Years of an African Slaver,*
New York, 1854

Schomburg Center for Research in Black Culture, Jean Blackwell Hutson Research and Reference Division, The New York Public Library. (1900). *Scene on the Coast; Branding a female slave.* Retrieved from http://digitalcollections.nypl.org/items/510d47df-9d3c-a3d9-e040-e00a18064a99

Plantation House

The "Big House" on a great Southern plantation.

Wattle and Daub Early Slave Dwelling

Schomburg Center for Research in Black Culture, Jean Blackwell Hutson Research and Reference Division, The New York Public Library. (1908). *Evolution of the Negro home; Slave - cabins, Southern United States [loaned by Southern Workman]*. Retrieved from http://digitalcollections.nypl.org/items/510d47df-3327-a3d9-e040-e00a18064a99

Slave Dwellings

NEGRO CABINS IN THE SOUTH, GIVING A FAIR IDEA OF "SLAVE QUARTERS."

Schomburg Center for Research in Black Culture, Jean Blackwell Hutson Research and Reference Division, The New York Public Library. (1925). *Negro cabins in the south, giving a fair idea of "slave quarters."* Retrieved from http://digitalcollections.nypl.org/items/510d47e4-7473-a3d9-e040-e00a18064a99

Circa Early 20th Century Slave Dwellings, Georgia

Underwood & Underwood. (ca. 1903) *Cabins where slaves were raised for market--The famous Hermitage, Savannah, Georgia.* Georgia Savannah, ca. 1903. New York: Underwood & Underwood, publishers. [Photograph] Retrieved from the Library of Congress, https://www.loc.gov/item/94505180/

Working the Cotton Fields

Schomburg Center for Research in Black Culture, Jean Blackwell
Hutson Research and Reference Division, the New York Public
Library. (1900). *As in Ante-bellum days*. Retrieved from
http://digitalcollections.nypl.org/items/510d47dd-f767-a3d9-
e040-e00a18064a99

Two Enslaved Boys

Slaves

Schomburg Center for Research in Black Culture, Photographs and Prints Division, the New York Public Library. (1850 - 1865). *Young boys* Retrieved from http://digitalcollections.nypl.org/items/510d47dc-4926-a3d9-e040-e00a18064a99

Runaway Slave

Schomburg Center for Research in Black Culture, Photographs and Prints Division, The New York Public Library. *Male adult slave escaping by way of a river.* Retrieved from http://digitalcollections.nypl.org/items/b024cc7d-b7d5-e1f4-e040-e00a18062e8d

Scourged for Running Away

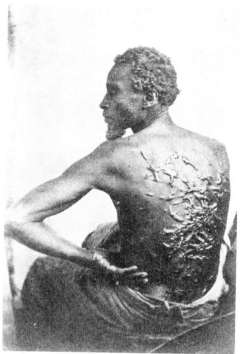

Schomburg Center for Research in Black Culture, Photographs and Prints Division, The New York Public Library. *The Scourged Back - The furrowed and scarred back of Gordon, a slave who escaped from his master in Mississippi and made his way to a Union Army encampment in Baton Rouge, Louisiana, 1863.* Retrieved from http://digitalcollections.nypl.org/items/510d47db-bc4e-a3d9-e040-e00a18064a99

Brutal Punishment: Death by Hanging, Thirst, and Hunger

Schomburg Center for Research in Black Culture, Jean Blackwell Hutson Research and Reference Division, The New York Public Library. (1910). *One of the atrocious methods of killing slaves pictured by Stedman; Hanging them up by a hook to die of thirst and famine.* Retrieved from http://digitalcollections.nypl.org/items/510d47df-8cf4-a3d9-e040-e00a18064a99

NOTE: It was customary to insert the hook under a rib to support the body and to extract maximum pain.

Slave Punishment: Common Method of Flogging used on all Slave Plantations

The mode of flogging Slaves.
as described in Bickells West Indies as they are. page 13.

Schomburg Center for Research in Black Culture, Photographs and Prints Division, The New York Public Library. (1829). *The mode of flogging Slaves, as described in Bickells "West Indies as they are."* Retrieved from http://digitalcollections.nypl.org/items/8991de20-2658-0132-1917-58d385a7b928

NOTE: When pregnant women were flogged in this manner, a hold was dug to accommodate the swollen belly.

Notice of Reward for Fugitive Slave

$200 Reward.

Ranaway from the subscriber, last
night, a mulatto man named FRANK MULLEN,
about twenty-one years old, five feet ten or eleven
inches high. He wears his hair long at the sides
and top, close behind, and keeps it nicely combed;
rather thick lips, mild countenance, polite when
spoken to, and very genteel in his person. His
clothing consists of a variety of summer and winter
articles, among which are a blue cloth coat and
blue casinet coatee, white pantaloons, blue cloth
do., and a pair of new ribbed casinet do., a blue
Boston wrapper, with velvet collar, several black
hats, boots, shoes, &c. As he has absconded without any provocation, it is presumed he will make
for Pennsylvania or New York. I will give one
hundred dollars if taken in the State of Maryland,
or the above reward if taken any where east of that
State, and secured so that I get him again, and all
reasonable expenses paid if brought home to the
subscriber, living in the city of Washington.

THOS. C. SCOTT.

October 21, 1835.

Restraints used on the Enslaved

No. 536. Iron Collar for Preventing the Escape of Slaves.

A WOMAN WITH IRON HORNS AND BELLS ON, TO KEEP HER
FROM RUNNING AWAY.

The New York Public Library. (1807). ["Log-yokes" to prevent slaves from escaping.] Retrieved from https://on.nypl.org/35sBVb7

144

Abolitionist Pamphlet: Announcement of Meeting

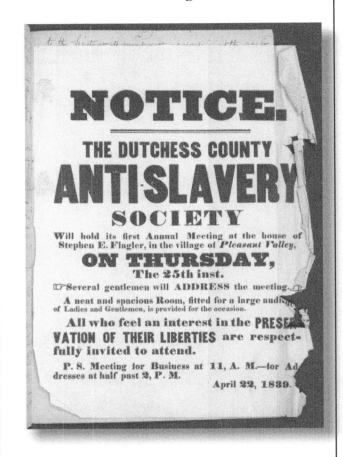

White Abolitionists Helping Fugitive Slaves

THE ROAD TO LIBERTY; A STATION ON THE UNDERGROUND RAILROAD.

Schomburg Center for Research in Black Culture, Photographs and Prints Division, The New York Public Library. *The Road to Liberty. A station on the Underground Railroad. (Escaped adults and children being convened from boat to waiting coach.)* Retrieved from https://on.nypl.org/34fGghT

Abolitionist Warning to Fugitive Slaves
(Boston, 1851)

CAUTION!!
COLORED PEOPLE
OF BOSTON, ONE & ALL,

You are hereby respectfully CAUTIONED and advised, to avoid conversing with the

Watchmen and Police Officers of Boston,

For since the recent ORDER OF THE MAYOR & ALDERMEN, they are empowered to act as

KIDNAPPERS
AND
Slave Catchers,

And they have already been actually employed in KIDNAPPING, CATCHING, AND KEEPING SLAVES. Therefore, if you value your LIBERTY, and the *Welfare of the Fugitives* among you, *Shun* them in every possible manner, as so many *HOUNDS* on the track of the most unfortunate of your race.

Keep a Sharp Look Out for KIDNAPPERS, and have TOP EYE open.
APRIL 24, 1851.

Schomburg Center for Research in Black Culture, Photographs and Prints Division, The New York Public Library. (1851). *Poster warning Blacks in Boston - kidnappers.* Retrieved from https://on.nypl.org/2OzzE7m

147

Frederick Douglass, 1845

Refugee Former Slaves in Canaan Land

A GROUP OF REFUGEE SETTLERS, OF WINDSOR, ONTARIO.
MRS. ANNE MARY JANE HUNT, MANSFIELD SMITH, MRS. LUCINDA SEYMOUR,
HENRY STEVENSON, BUSH JOHNSON.
(From a recent photograph.)

Schomburg Center for Research in Black Culture, Photographs and Prints Division, The New York Public Library. *A group of refugee settlers, of Windsor, Ontario. Mrs. Anne Mary Jane Hunt, Manfield Smith, Mrs. Lucinda Seymour.* Retrieved from https://on.nypl.org/35yhD09

UPCOMING WORKS

Original Works of Poetry: Traditional and Japanese style tanka and haiku poems. [Due for release in 2020]

Apocalyptic: A sobering tale of how the children of Lucifer, from the lineage of Cain and identified in John 8:44, continue to wage war against the One True God, YHWH, through politics, race, and religion. Do they know who they are, and is there a way to recognize them in the 21st century? How do they fit into the Creator's plan for the Rapture event? [Due for release in 2021]

Historical Fiction: Paranormal tale set in the antebellum South. [Due for release in 2021]

Religious: The pagan roots of some popular Christian celebrations are examined in light of John 4: 24. [Due for release in 2020]

Works from the Public Domain: Classics, religious, and sacred texts revised and reformatted for the 21st-century book-lover. Enlightened readers, students, and scholars will appreciate these versions, which are being updated with annotations, commentaries, and illustrations. [Due for release starting in 2020]

Contact: tappinbooks@aol.com
Facebook: www.facebook.com/rmtappinauthor
Website: www.rmtappin.net
Twitter: www.twitter.com/rmtappin_author
[Blog coming soon at: rmtappinauthor.com]

COVER DESIGN

Designer: Charaf Essbati

Contact Information:

-facebook.com/coverssyart
-essbaticharafpay@gmail.com
-essbaticharaf@coverssy.com
-coverssy.com

Made in the USA
Coppell, TX
17 December 2021